WHERE RAINBOWS BEGIN

SEASONS OF THE JOURNEY

BY

DONALD J BRADY

DEDICATED TO

WANDA NELL WILSON BRADY

MY DEAR MOTHER AND FRIEND

Special Thanks To

Phyllis A McNeill

Who boldly led the way on many desert safaris

Each journey begins at a given place where time and eternity briefly embrace. Every season in life's great scroll colors our canvas of living gold. I grew up in the wild west days of atomic testing not far from the famed Nevada Test Site and radioactive lore. As a young boy, I often explored a stark yet alluring desert frontier where each bold day brought grand adventure. Early life in a southwestern desert amidst curious critters of every kind, colored those days with marvelous wonder. This is a rich story of discovery as seen through the eyes of a growing boy who later in life became blind. It's the true story of a mother's enduring love and the living rainbows that shimmered through soft summer rains and sudden storms. Come with me on a gem lined journey through endearing passages of time and upward rocky climbs, where skyward colors touched the land … to a place where rainbows began.

Contents

Our Indian Springs Summer

A song of rain in the great southwest can wake a land from lonesome rest. As thirsty rocks receive the rain, a bow appears and life begins…

Wanda Wilson came from the warm Panhandle of Texas to the hot frying pan of Las Vegas in 1954. She occasionally turned on the radio while driving to her new job at the remote Nevada Proving Grounds. As atomic testing rocked the early Las Vegas area, a guy called Elvis was creating shock waves across the radio. Yet Wanda was more shook up over a young lieutenant of security she met in the atomic wild west. Now William J Brady was not the same sheriff who got shot by Billy the Kid, but rather a bold officer with a burnished badge who helped tame an atomic frontier. "Jay" and Wanda's first date was a shake and bake event as they viewed an atomic blast at sunrise. They held each other's hand as a gentle countdown began, then a fireball lit the sky. It was more than a spark that brought them together, so they walked down an aisle of hope and heather. Jay and Wanda joined hands forever on June 18, 1955 at Little Church of the West in Las Vegas. Judy Garland would also marry there … at a place where rainbows began.

Jay and Wanda began to have kids as couples sometimes do. Phyllis and Linda joined the show as stars in bobby sock shoes. Now mother and dad wanted a boy who could dig in the dirt and add to the joy. Donnie arrived on a bright summer day with buckets of love and more on the way. That's how we all became the Brady Bunch. Mother brought me home from the hospital in Las Vegas to a small ranch house at Indian Springs. Some nearby geese thought I was an odd-looking duck as mother set me by the spring fed pond. Even a flock of gobbling turkeys gandered over for a curious look. Indian Springs was a small place, but in August of 1960 it became my new Eden on earth.

Now dad could design something at breakfast and have it built before sundown. He lived in a time where tools were a man's best friend. The desert cottage he built for us on Sky Road was small indeed but seemed like a mansion to me. The foundation was so strong that even nearby atomic testing couldn't shake it. Maybe it was the special sand dad gathered from spent missile nose cones that created such immovable cement. Our windows were small but gave us a view of life on eternity's edge.

Dad often drove to nearby Mercury, Nevada where he first arrived as a security pioneer. I guess atomic testing just flowed through his bones, like honey from bees in hexagonal homes. He helped secure sensitive areas for visits by President Kennedy and other key guests through the years. Dad also provided special services at home when we called for vital assistance. Somehow, I fell off the bed one night as my large head greeted a lampstand below. Wailing cries pierced the calm night as Phyllis and Linda were the first to arrive. Donnie hit his head they mournfully said as dad turned on a light. He assessed the trauma and announced I would probably survive. Then mother stretched forth her sure arms of safety and tearfully said, "I just want to hold my baby."

I always felt safe in mother's arms as she lifted me up to the kitchen counter. A cheerful lamb cookie jar with a ceramic straw hat waited there with a forever smile. Upon lifting the golden hat, a gleeful lamb's baa heralded a happy harvest within. Mother set me across the counter and eased my head towards the sink for a good old-fashioned hair washing. I then noticed some red and white cupid candy near the smiling cookie jar.

What's that? I curiously asked.

Those are some special treats and you can have some when we're all done.

That seemed like a good deal to me, so we proceeded with the soapy process.

I wasn't much taller than a tumbleweed when mother and dad got me a real western outfit. I wore small blue jeans with a big sky shirt, a cowboy vest and chaps, even a pair of rugged boots and thirsty two-gallon hat. A couple quick toy guns with double holsters gave added authority to my deputy star badge. I could well have walked some distant streets even as Marshal Matt Dillon. There was also my trusted riding horse, mounted on sturdy springs. You could almost ride him forever and he never got tired till you did. Now mother had a movie camera that filmed in living color. She pulled it from a holster as I drew and ducked for cover. I'm not sure who was faster that day, a smiling mother or me, as I ran to reach her outstretched hands in a summer at Indian Springs.

Tricycles can generate excitement in every child's life. We had two such three-wheeled critters and rode them with great delight. Phyllis and Linda had already blazed several tricycle trails around our frontier drive by the time I was old enough to mount up and ride. One trike looked weary and spent like a Pony Express steed at journey's end. The other sparkled a pristine blue with a large front wheel and tassels too. Sweet grips rose above a custom seat and with two steps in back it was showroom complete. This was the Cadillac of tricycles and maybe I could ride it someday.

The grand cement drive that dad built could surely have rivaled the Speedway at Indianapolis. There with our Radio Flyer wagon, the girls and I gathered some neighbor kids for an epic event. Some of the greatest racing spectacles ever witnessed occurred in our own front yard at the famed Indian Springs Speedway. Our faithful red wagon was always ready for action. Actually, it had more of a reddish-brown sun baked patina and appeared to have rolled along several heat soaked miles of Route 66. Mother sometimes brought a garden hose to our beloved wagon and filled it to the brim. Phyllis and I then splashed among a desert oasis within.

Our little house on Sky Road was a big part of early life. Yet, now that I was four, it was time to see more of what lay beyond. The wild desert was full of wonder on an Indian Springs afternoon.

Mother, can I go outside to play?

Yes Donnie, but be careful, I don't want anything to happen to my little boy.

While bounding along a desert pathway, I somehow found myself hurtling towards earth and experiencing the full force of gravity. In a universe of rocks below, I landed head first among them. One of those angular stones struck my forehead and much like Goliath, I was down for the count. My dented noggin really hurt as bright red droplets sprinkled around me. I eventually returned to mother for some much needed comfort and care.

What happened Donnie–are you hurt? Let me see your forehead. She held a cool washcloth over my wound and quickly drove to a local doctor who had just opened a practice. Mother carried me up some long steps and inside an unusual place with yellow walls. Just looking at those walls made me feel unwell. The doctor set me on top of something and wore a large bright light around his head. Mother watched with worry as he cleaned and closed the wound with stitches. He was a kind man, yet I was glad when all was done. I guess things just happen sometimes and the best we can do is help them heal as we go on.

Donnie, would you like to go with me into town?

Yes mother, I want to go with you.

Las Vegas was about 45 miles from Indian Springs and most grocery stores were located there. I could just see over the dashboard as we drove by sloping desert vistas. An occasional Joshua Tree seemed to point the way. Along the road, colorful bottles lay scattered among thirsty creosote and yucca. Some appeared to have been there many seasons, others untold years.

Are we there yet? I patiently asked.

Almost, she assured me.

We'll each have a popsicle after we're done shopping.

Radio towers began to appear in the distance and then a few buildings as we got closer to town. There it was! The giant T atop a towering Thriftimart sign. You couldn't miss it, even in an airplane. The parking lot sure was big with deep rows of cars and trucks. Hold my hand and stay close Donnie, some of the drivers may not be able to see you.

Mother set me in the grocery cart but sometimes I walked alongside as she did the shopping. Almost everywhere we went, someone would say to mother, "he sure is cute!" I think that made both of us feel good. Through the years I've secretly hoped that people would keep saying that about me.

Mother and I both enjoyed a cold popsicle on the way home. I usually had an orange or grape flavor, but banana was my favorite.

Up the desert hills from Indian Springs and not so far away, a road rises toward cathedral peaks and ponderosa pine. There in the crisp air of an early autumn, mother held me, breathing in the beauty that surrounded us. Stately aspen trees with leaves of living gold shimmered across the meadow. It was here, among alpine vistas of the Toiyobe Forest, that mother and dad decided to build a summer cabin. Dad's mountain man dream was grand indeed. Family and friends could come together in a great homegrown effort. He and mother would stand at the helm, but even our little hands could help. Dad then conceived a two story A-frame cabin that was born to live in mountain splendor.

Lee Canyon was a natural wonder just waiting to be loved. I believe alpine air may be the oxygen of heaven with the fragrance thereof. My tiny nose turned in every direction trying to find a source of that pleasant aroma, then realized it was everywhere. I scampered among smiling ponderosa and scooped up precious fallen pinecones. Such jewels of the forest adorned every rocky hillside. Soft Indian Paintbrush petals caressed my little fingers with mutual delight. A moving sea of stars then danced above our campfire as they joyously celebrated each new night. In less than a year, we finished our summer cabin at Lee Canyon. It soon embraced and warmed us with ever glowing light.

Christmas at Indian Springs brushed the days of December with noble fir and the night with soft twinkling lights. Mother and dad decorated our home with simple and beautiful things. We opened our presents on Christmas Eve and dad was excited with what I received. The new Lionel electric train set just needed a full-time engineer and that would be me.

The front locomotive was large and strong, coupled with a fully laden coal car. A flat rail transport carried my Lincoln Logs as a forest green passenger car trailed along. A brave red caboose then followed them all. Electric track sections were joined to create oval and figure 8 designs. When a transformer switched on, the great train travelled a wonderous track in one continuous round. The imagination and wide eyes of a small boy, along with those of his young at heart dad, followed that train of smiles for many seasons to come. It always pulled a car of dreams and lighter load of cares.

The early days at Indian Springs bloomed and quickly passed, like butterflies in a summer breeze they came and fluttered back. I tried to catch them in my hands and hold them to my heart, where dreams are born and songs begin, a place where rainbows start.

The First Time

Moving from our cottage home at Indian Springs was like saying goodbye to a dear friend. We all kept some emotional artwork from the place where early life began. Yet our new home on El Camino Road in Las Vegas felt like the Ponderosa Ranch compared to the humble homestead we just left. In 1964, the new place stood like a lone cypress on the remote edge of town. Dad was eager to place his signature on the home's modern entryway and did so with a dazzling rock face planter. You see, dad was a Michelangelo of rockwork and created a centerpiece of mica schist and sparkling stones. Every rock he set was just where it needed to be in the universe. My young eyes were transfigured and beheld a glittering galaxy in every precious stone.

Now everyone had a favorite blanket while growing up and I still do. Around the fabulous age of four, a soft green quilt was my ever-present guardian. Wherever I bravely went, my comforting quilt was a robe of flowing splendor. If I fell asleep in front of the tv, mother would carefully guide me and the trailing quilt back to my room. As mother placed me in bed, I could gaze towards a peaceful nightlight.

Donnie, would you like to say a prayer with me before I go?

Yes mother … how do we pray?

Just follow me and we'll say the words together.

Now I lay me down to sleep, Lord I pray my soul to keep,

If I die before I wake, Lord I pray my soul to take.

Did we say it good? I whispered.

Yes, Donnie, we did just fine.

Mother's face seemed to glow a little in the soft evening light. I watched as she then passed through an open door to rest for the night.

Dad was sometimes thought to be a genius. One of his best ideas was to surprise me with a new pedal car. Mother said he sat for hours with a bucket of tools trying to assemble the mechanical wonder. During the process, he often declared the dumbo engineers had designed it all wrong. Perhaps the Wright Brothers attempting to assemble their plane for a first flight at Kitty Hawk could best compare. Dad's persistence finally prevailed as a mechanized marvel rolled forth into our family showroom.

We have a surprise for you, Donnie.

Cover your eyes and don't peek yet.

Ready, now open your eyes and see.

It's a car! I hollered, clapping with instant approval.

There stood a sleek snow-white pedal car with red flames of fire rising on each side.

It's for you, Donnie.

Can I sit in it?

Go ahead, but be careful not to run into the furniture. Tomorrow you can drive it all you want outside.

Well, tomorrow did come and my first new car was already idling with excitement.

Let's go to the front, mother said as she led the way.

Dad moved the full-size family car and cleared the circular drive. I carefully positioned myself on the sturdy metal seat while firmly gripping a responsive steering wheel. My four year old feet pressed quickly upon pedals of destiny. Ignition!

I generated an incredible amount of power and appeared to be pulling G's while accelerating around the circular drive. Dad was astonished at the amazing kinetic energy on display. This was a fast car. The sizzling flames on each side panel testified to that.

I soon realized that my new pedal car performed best with a special blend of high-octane sugar, which I dutifully provided. Every few laps around the curving drive brought another checkered flag and taste of glory. I often found myself, as A. J. Foyt, in a winner's circle of champions. Mother had fun filming her new racing legend and dad applauded the dreams of a small boy as we celebrated together. Could there be an endless acknowledgment and special awards for all who complete the most challenging course called life? Yes, as the sun rises and surely sets, comes a resounding refrain of Yes.

Laguna Beach is a charming coastal city, a pearl peeking through California's southern seascape. Grandma Ann and Grandpa Earnie enjoyed living there for a brief season in life. Visiting them was always a treasured experience. Our family of five, Wanda and Jay, Phyllis, Linda and Donnie, was like a five flavor group of Fruit Stripe gum and each had a different taste. Yet all looked forward to experiencing the full flavor of California's pacific ocean. This was a seaside feast for the senses compared to Nevada's dry toast desert.

Rhythmic aqua waves welcomed us at Laguna Beach. Pleasant aromas drifted freely with a soft sea breeze. Each new breath of living ocean air seemed to celebrate the vitality of life. Ribbons of rich kelp adorned the shoreline, flowing with each rising tide. Rushing waves often carried a cargo of colorful seashells. Gathering the castaway shells was like a joyful Easter egg hunt by the sea. We realized the original owners probably didn't need them anymore. Savvy seabirds watched eagerly as each approaching wave brought a potential beachfront buffet. The harvest truly was great and it was a good time to be a bird. An undiscovered universe swirled around my toes in each tidepool. My finger could draw on a surf swept canvas in glistening grains of sand. Gentle waves brimming with seafoam then washed upon my delightful creations. Like an ebb tide etch a sketch, a perfect palette would soon reappear.

A generation later, I invited Linda's children, Heidi and Blake, to experience an ocean for the first time. There at Laguna Beach, they frolicked in the surf, explored some tidepools and created designs in the sand. In every generation of time, our loving oceans and healing waters invite all to join in her endless dance of life.

My fifth birthday was a gala event. Grandma Ann and Grandpa Earnie invited us to come visit, which I thought was a fine idea. Grandparents have a wonderful way of helping everyone feel loved. A western themed swirl cake was set before us on their table. Several Cowboys and Indians were planted knee-deep in frosting atop a colorful cake mesa. They had evidently reached a peace treaty before the cake was made and were fully ready to celebrate with us. Sometimes we played Cowboys and Indians at home, not Cowboys and Native Americans. We never heard of political correctness and the notion that something political could be correct, well, just didn't make sense.

Make a wish, everyone chimed. Five flickering candles stood before me as I took a full breath and certain aim. Little did I realize how soon fifty would be added to those five.

What did you wish for? Grandma teased.

Maybe that someone named Donald J will be President someday, Grandpa suggested.

Mother and dad congratulated me on a milestone birthday as cousin Dean and I began to play. Suddenly, I turned around to find a half-century had passed that way.

Time to wake up, Donnie. Today is your first day of school, mother eagerly said.

I'll help you get ready.

Kindergarten was going to be a step up in the world. The excitement of seeing new kids, the application of interpersonal skills, playtime management, this was almost like beginning a new job.

I made this lunch for you and wrote your name on the bag, mother assured me. Let's go out front and wait for the bus.

The yellow school bus was easy to see, even in the distance. Like an approaching bumble bee, the yellow creature with black stripes droned ever closer. The bus doors opened to reveal some mighty big steps. This was like boarding a locomotive. I sat by a window and watched as mother waved goodbye.

Doris Hancock was a new elementary school in 1965. Our kindergarten teacher, Mrs. Tiesenhausen, welcomed and encouraged us to befriend one another. The first classroom roll call found my name near the top.

Here! I hollered.

Yes Donald, but not so loud, the new teacher implored.

OK, I whispered.

One poor fellow, whose last name began with the letter Z, was forever doomed to be the last person called on every roll.

There was story time, where the teacher read from a good book and we sat as devoted disciples. There was play time, when a variety of wood building blocks tumbled among us. Mrs. Tiesenhausen invited us to team up with another child and build something special. My partner and I quickly gathered twelve of the largest blocks. I stacked them as high as we could, then built steps surrounding our engineering marvel. I'm not sure if it met building code specs, but I climbed up and sat atop the towering structure. Our teacher then roamed the room visiting each pair of kids and their imaginative creations.

Donald, what did you build? she curiously asked.

It's a motorcycle, I proudly declared.

I see, well you be careful up there.

Then there was naptime, which was also a handy break time for the teacher. Once all the kids were corralled, everyone could enjoy a well deserved siesta.

We sometimes sat at small tables where generous rewards of Play-Doh were bestowed upon us. I made clay birds, cats, dogs, elephants, fish, giraffes and horses. If we pooled our clay resources together, there was even enough to build an ark. Special recognition was given to each child who could eventually recite from memory their parent's names, home address and telephone number. For us, this was like reaching the rank of Lt. Colonel.

Well, graduation day from kindergarten cheerfully arrived with an early summer breeze. Mother said I looked handsome wearing the small white shirt and clip-on tie she got for the special ceremony. Mrs. Tiesenhausen, our principal and other dignitaries welcomed everyone to the happy occasion. The outdoor stage and viewing area saw many proud parents watch as their treasured children marched forward to receive individual diplomas. Mother brought her Kodak home movie camera and filmed the historic event in technicolor. Everyone enjoyed some richly frosted graduation cake and I felt like a coronated king.

Look mother, someone made a pretty rainbow over there.

How far away is it?

Not very far, Donnie.

Mother then hugged me for a moment.

Can we go towards the rainbow? I asked.

Maybe someday we'll go there together, she smiled.

Every Easter, mother hopped around our house hiding colorful candy treats. There were green, blue, purple, white, red, orange and yellow, just about every color of the rainbow marshmallows. Phyllis, Linda and I each carried a handwoven Easter basket as we scampered through the house gathering tasty treats. Chocolate bunnies rustled in our baskets amid speckled robin eggs and flavorful jelly beans. Sometimes mother gave us clues if we searched too far from the hidden treasures.

Phyllis, you're warm, getting warmer, almost there.

Donnie, you're really warm, almost hot.

There it is! A small packet of jelly beans just waiting for an owner.

Once the Easter egg harvest was complete, we bounded towards a sweet laden feast. Chocolate bunnies were usually the first to go. Legs were bitten, delicate ears nibbled and candy eyes gobbled. A variety of chocolate covered eggs were also favored. Everything was received with delicious love. Mother planted some candy in such good hiding places that it continued to spring forth even weeks later. Wanda was a wonderful mother and special friend, even sweeter than Willy Wonka.

The Easter candy sure tasted good and mother reminded me to brush my teeth each day. Well, one of my small front teeth became loose and was almost ready to come out. Someone described taking a pair of pliers and gently yanking it out. That didn't sound very good. Another friend instructed me to tie one end of a string around the loose tooth and the other end around a door handle, then quickly slam the door shut. That really didn't sound good. I sat contemplating a better strategy, while unwrapping a blue candy-coated Easter egg. As I bit down on the crunchy treat, my little tooth popped right out. What a sweet surprise! If you ever have a loose tooth that needs to come out, may I recommend the candy Easter egg method. It hurts less and tastes better too.

Look mother, my loose tooth fell out!

Maybe you should leave it for the Tooth Fairy, she said.

Who's the Tooth Fairy?

Well, the Tooth Fairy comes to get your teeth when they fall out.

What does she do with them?

She saves them, mother explained.

Maybe you should leave the tooth under your pillow tonight and see what happens.

Ok, will the Tooth Fairy know where to come, I wondered aloud.

I think she knows, mother smiled.

That night I placed the small pearl tooth under my pillow as excitement bubbled around me. Maybe I would see the Tooth Fairy come, what should I do? A little later, mother came by to check on me and I'm glad she did.

In the morning, the little tooth was gone and 75 cents shone brightly before my eyes. What a wonderful surprise. I began to count how many more teeth I had and if any of them were loose.

Donnie, did you find anything under your pillow this morning?

Yes mother, 75 cents!

I want to thank the Tooth Fairy, but how can I do it?

I'll let her know, mother softly said with a smile.

Mother sure knew a lot about things and I was thankful to be with her.

First grade was a time of many firsts for me. Most of the kids were about six years of age, but our teacher, Mrs. Osguthorpe, was a bit older. Here was the first time I kissed a girl. Natalie was standing near a classroom door when I gave her the most wonderful smooch. She giggled at the fun of it all and her lips tasted like a flavorful burst of orange. Actually, she had been enjoying a large naval orange and I could tell it was delicious.

I got my first pair of glasses in first grade. Mother realized I couldn't see things very well, especially on a classroom board. I was so nearsighted that new glasses helped me feel almost born again. Now don't pay attention to any kids who may call you four eyes, I was told. Well, my new glasses were like looking through the Hubble telescope for the first time and the other kids treated me just fine.

First grade was also the first time I embraced the sport of judo. Mother received an invitation, as other parents did, to enroll their kids in after school judo classes.

Donnie, would you like to learn judo?

Her eyes sparkled with curious wonder.

Yes mother, then I can be your bodyguard.

My judo gi and white belt of honor became welcome friends in this new world of wisdom and inner strength. As young students, we practiced a multitude of judo moves, throws and falls. We were introduced to an almost endless sea of judo mats that rolled before us. I quickly learned it was better to fall on top of someone rather than underneath. Each class concluded with a mutual bow among students and teacher.

At home, I invited Phyllis and Linda to help demonstrate some of my favorite judo moves and throws, but they were reluctant to participate. Upon successful completion of several enlightening and energetic classes, our jewel of judo experience continued to shine. Perhaps, if we can grapple with challenges, wrestle with adversity and overcome falls, we'll almost always come through on top.

First grade was the first time I got sent to the principal's office. I must have teased one of the other kids and the teacher wasn't very pleased. On the lonely walk to meet the principal, I considered my options. Would I confess, how should I plead? The school secretary met and directed me to Mr. Englehart's office. There was a big desk, a really big desk, with a large chair of authority on the other side.

The principal will be in shortly, she said.

I sat in a small chair and quickly bowed my head. Upon closing my eyes, I began to offer a quiet yet fervent prayer.

God, please don't let me be in trouble.

I promise to be good.

I'll be good forever.

It was a prayer for the ages.

Suddenly, I heard a voice. Unbeknownst to me, Mr. Englehart had quietly entered the room and was now sitting in his chair. I can't remember what he said, but there was to be no jail time or public record. I was given a fresh start and felt like a new man.

I've tried to keep my promise since that solemn day, but have surely stumbled many times along the rocky way. I hope the Lord is ever kind, as Mr. Englehart could be, when I go to see Him someday, may He look and smile at me.

Second grade was a welcome promotion and time of philosophical freedom. School was mostly fun and carefree, but I sometimes became a bit unruly. Dad firmly encouraged me to straighten up which I promptly did. Mother always put good things in my lunch pail before I rambled off each morning, but she was also a favorite lunchtime pal. We sometimes met in front of school and sallied forth to McDonalds for a happy midday meal. I always had a tasty hamburger, fry and small orange drink. Mother and I talked about many things and a bright future ahead. The burger and fries were sure good, but lunchtimes with mother were best.

My second favorite time, recess on the playground, was a fun filled free-for-all. The ever popular jungle gym and monkey bars served as early training for possible SEAL TEAM service. It's amazing how most of us survived those rough and tumble days. When necessary, a heroic school nurse patched us up pretty well. The most effective first aid treatment was often an ice cream sandwich. Mother understood this and gave me a daily dime for the comforting necessity.

Mother was also a pretty good medic and rescued me more than a few times. Indoor sprinting, also known as running in the house, was my premier track and field event. At just seven years of age, I was on a record setting pace down the hallway. A sure medal and great honor awaited when I suddenly tripped on a loose blanket that some goofball (me) left strewn in my pathway to glory. The racing baton I held, a foot long ruler, sheared off as I struck the floor. The shattered wood met my face with bullseye accuracy. This crash of the century left me dazed and reeling. Mother heard my moans and quickly came to the scene.

Let me look at you, she instantly said.

Mother grabbed a damp washcloth and pressed upon the fresh wound. The jagged ruler had struck my face precisely on the right corner of my beautiful mouth.

Better get you to a doctor or hospital right away, she insisted.

Please God, help my face get better.

I looked towards mother as she speedily drove and quietly said, I'll be ok.

Someone stitched the wound and told mother how fortunate I had been as she sighed with relief. I then wore the hospital bandage as a true badge of honor and still wear a small scar on the corner of my mouth. My smile is just a little longer on the right side. Over time, I've found it better to not run with rulers and also to let scars become smiles.

Now riding a bike is easy, once you know how to do it. I had often watched my sisters propel themselves on two-wheeled camels to far away places. Having reached the full age of seven, it was time to receive my bicycle baptism. Linda's bicycle had already given years of faithful service. Her once bright pony appeared worn and weary. Years ago, it gallantly trod the Chisholm Trail. Now it leaned with arthritic joints in a dusty desert stable. Yet, the lonely bike spoke to me in that warm summer breeze. Get on my young friend, you can always ride me.

I guess riding a bicycle is similar to riding a horse. Each steers a bit differently and one requires less pedaling than the other. Also, it hurts a little less to fall off a bicycle than a horse. I carefully mounted the sun-baked bike and bravely balanced on both black pedals. After several tries and as many flops, I amazingly remained upright. Further and further I rode. A rush of freedom flowed through handlebar streamers and my new butch haircut. Mother cheered me on as I showcased phenomenal riding skills. Keep going, keep going, she urged. Like Old Glory, the faded red bike and I rolled on.

Our first cat was a beautiful Blue Point Siamese. He simply came to the front door and walked right in. We gave the friendly visitor a bowl of fresh milk and he purred like a motor boat. Dad let the lovable cat stay and named him Rama. We soon discovered our adopted guest was out of this world smart. When Rama wanted to go outside, he sat by the front door and meowed. If his request was not soon met, he would jump to the door handle and turn it with his paws. Sometimes we found the sliding back door open and couldn't figure how it was so. One day, I happened to spy Rama in action. He jumped on top of a reclining chair and reached toward the sliding door. He steadily lifted the locking latch and pushed the slider open. Rama held the best universal key in his own paws.

Now Phyllis had drawn a colorful sketch of Rudolph the Red-Nosed Reindeer for Christmas. She placed it above our small piano and attached a bright red ornament for its nose. Rama sat staring at the irresistible ornament and portrait on the wall. Suddenly, he leapt atop the piano and took great delight in removing Rudolph's nose. Each time we replaced the shiny red ball, he became more determined to retrieve and play with it. Rama was simply a stellar genius. We're not sure where Rama really came from, but he often sat outside at night, gazing toward the stars.

The first time I stayed at a hospital was to have my tonsils removed. I didn't volunteer for the procedure, but a doctor from the Civil War era convinced my parents that having them removed could bring peace to an ongoing sore throat conflict. Dad said I would probably survive the operation and promised to come see me at the hospital if I did. I offered Linda my favorite Super Ball if I didn't.

Mother held my hand as the hospital folks came to whisk me away.

Donnie, everything will be alright and I'll be waiting for you, she smiled.

The rolling bed was kind of noisy and people there always seemed to be in a hurry. The operating room had some really bright lights and all the nurses wore shower caps. I looked at the ceiling for a while and made a silent wish.

Please God, if You're there, don't let me die today, I don't want to leave mother.

We're going to give you some ether, a nurse with pretty glasses said.

They gently placed a thick yellow mask over my mouth and nose.

Just relax and breathe.

I fussed a little and told that nurse the air didn't taste very good.

It's ok to just blow it away, she assured me.

Well, I took several deep breaths and blew like a storm. It must have worked because I didn't remember much after that.

I woke up in another room but sure had a sore throat. Mother came in to see me and I began to feel better. Another nurse came by with some vital instructions from the doctor. I could have as much ice cream and sherbet as I wanted. I accepted the doctor's wise guidance and became convinced of his expertise. An angel nurse then showed me a secret ice cream call button, which I sometimes pressed during a sherbet emergency. There was orange, grape, pineapple, strawberry, lemon and even rainbow sherbet. It was good medicine and I enjoyed several refills.

Dad came by the next day and brought his chess set. We played a bit before he grasped my small hand in his strong one.

See you again soon, he waved.

I did return home and got to keep my Super Ball. It bounced above some angel wings and sometimes even higher, then rolled beside a rocky road and hid within a briar. I lost it once among some clouds, but it came back to me, like people who you always love and swallows in the spring.

The first indoor mall of Las Vegas and perhaps even Nevada opened with much acclaim in early 1968. Mother and dad decided to go see for themselves what all the hoopla was about and invited me to tag along. We arrived at the impressive Boulevard Mall and made our way towards the grand entrance.

Hold my hand, I don't want you to get lost, mother said.

We suddenly entered an indoor city of bright lights and crystalline windows. Mother especially wanted to visit the much talked about Broadway store. Mother and dad soon deposited me upstairs in the vital toy department as they browsed the less interesting furniture and houseware areas. We would meet again at a later appointed time. I roamed an entire second floor and ultimately tamed the Broadway wilderness.

Some time passed, whether hours or years, I'm not sure. Suddenly, the bright lights went dim and the great store became dark. Something must be closing, but where were mother and dad? Had they wandered off somewhere? I found a tall escalator which was silent and no longer moving. Well pardner, I guess it's just me on the upper range now, but where are the stars? In the twilight, I set up camp on the second floor, near the top of a quiet escalator. More time passed, then the silhouette of someone appeared in the distance below.

Are you Donnie? A voice echoed.

Yes, I replied.

Your parents are looking for you, the assistant manager relayed.

Ok, I'm coming down now.

Can you see alright to come down the escalator steps?

Yes sir, I'm a good climber.

Your parents will be glad to see you, he assured me, and they were.

I realized that quiet night in Broadway, how good it was to always keep an eye on your parents, so they don't get lost.

My first camera created colorful fingerprints of time. What beautiful things could I photograph? The desert swirled with caramel and cinnamon browns. Our rosemary plants were nice, but we also needed some active wildlife. My favorite cat Peter volunteered to play the special part. He stood majestically among tall grass as I readied the camera. Look this way Peter and give me that meow moment. That's a take. Now turn west, as if on a wild safari. Excellent. Together we created an impressive portfolio of Peter the Great.

There must be more.

I gathered an array of antique bottles that had been waiting for such a time as this. Amber, ruby and violet glass glistened in the grateful light. The desert sky then blossomed with a vivid southwestern sunset. Da Vinci couldn't have painted it better. My first roll of film was complete. Our eyes beheld a panorama of living color, my camera, a few brief moments in the golden vista of time.

Breakfast With Grandma

I discovered early in life that grandparents were simply perfect. Grandma Ann and Grandpa Earnie gave heartfelt hugs and were always glad to see us. Grandma thought the world of mother and often spoke of how fortunate her son Jay was to have found her. Grandpa stood tall in every way and his hands were marked with kindness. Everyone was glad when they came to visit. Phyllis, Linda and I also welcomed the traditional tub of treats that Grandma always brought and we quickly gave it a good home. A variety of mini chocolate bars swam in a sea of bobbing jelly beans just waiting to be rescued. All these provided daily strength to meet the many challenges of childhood.

During one of their visits, I noticed a pretty head of hair resting among Grandma's things.

What's that? I asked.

Oh, that's just a wig I sometimes wear.

Why?

Well, if my own hair isn't fixed up yet, I can just wear that, she explained.

Can I try it on?

You'll look silly if you wear that, Donnie.

Let me put it on and I'll go get my guitar.

Ok, Grandma laughed, but I should get a photo of this.

I placed the long brunette hair over my recent crew cut. We added one of those colorful Hawaiian leis that Grandma had brought for Phyllis. I shouldered my full-size guitar and stood in bright red swim trunks, ready to dazzle the adoring crowds.

You look like a little Elvis, Grandma hollered, while capturing the Kodak moment.

Maybe I could become a music legend.

Then dad walked by with a wrinkled frown and didn't seem to approve of my flowing hair.

So, I quickly made a necessary career change.

Phyllis and Linda had previously stayed with Grandma and Grandpa at their home in Burbank, Ca for two wonderful weeks. I was about seven years old and now man enough to do the same. This was the first time I flew alone, but the nice stewardesses with TWA kept a close eye on me. They soon guided me forward to meet our friendly captain. He invited me to sit in his chair and I even held the airplane steering wheel shortly before takeoff. I wonder if Toren, who is Phyllis' grandson and now about the same age as I was then, may someday wear such a captain's hat and pilot a similar airborne craft.

Well, Grandma faithfully waited, met and whisked me away from a bustling California airport. We soon arrived at a quaint cottage on East Orange Grove in Burbank. Grandma and Grandpa's lovely little home seemed to embrace everyone. I eagerly tromped up the front steps and claimed it as my own. Soft shades of chiffon green and pacific blue caressed each relaxing room. Any worries that someone carried didn't seem to fit through their small front door. I slept well that night and life was perfect indeed.

Morning found me as a hungry hound following a savory scent. My faithful nose tracked it to Grandma's diner style kitchen. Sizzling bacon framed a warm plate of sunny side up eggs that seemed to smile. Crispy ears of buttered toast along with fruit flavored jellies surrounded my morning feast. I quickly felt like king for a day with Grandma's love along the way.

Did you enjoy breakfast? she asked with a smile.

How do you spell delicious twice? I quickly replied.

Now Grandma and I were not alone in the kitchen. She and Grandpa had an adorable poodle named Mitzi. She seemed to especially enjoy the kitchen area and intently watched all activities therein. Looking up, Mitzi gazed upon Grandma, while tilting her head. The poodle mind is a beautiful thing and she contemplated what tasty morsels might soon appear. Drizzling bacon was a snack of royalty and Mitzi had already been crowned Duchess of Burbank.

Good morning Mitzi, I am Duke Donnie of Las Vegas. I gently lifted her long soft ears to discover an intricate sound system capable of easily detecting any visitors who came up the walkway. Mitzi always had a warm welcome for the mailman. There was excitement when greeting family and friends. A slightly different response came for door knocking salesmen and politicians. Grandma, Grandpa and Mitzi enjoyed watching a little tv at night. I noticed that if a political speech was aired, they turned it down and gave more attention to Mitzi. I began to wonder if pets were more important than politicians.

This was the home where my dad Jay had lived during the 1940's. He was born on June 14, Flag Day, and like many young men of that great generation, felt a deep respect for that flag of honor. Dad wanted to serve His Country and chose the U.S. Navy to do so. Before Jay's Burbank High School graduation ceremonies had even occurred, he was already stationed in San Diego. As so many parents did during that time, Grandma and Grandpa displayed a small Son in Service sign in the window of their home. Dad set sail from San Diego and served aboard the USS Raymond as it patrolled the South Pacific. Jay sometimes steered the ship and served with honor for the remaining short duration of World War 2.

Shortly after returning home from service, dad stayed with Ann and Earnie back at Burbank. He just wasn't feeling well and his temperature quickly rose. During the night, Jay began to cough blood and stumbled towards his parent's room. He reached for their door and was able to call one word, "dad" as he collapsed to the floor. Earnie somehow heard a noise and found Jay just in time. Dad had double pneumonia and his lungs were hemorrhaging. Doctors weren't sure if he'd pull through. It was touch and go for several days as Jay lay in a hospital for two weeks. Dad did survive and later said he thought angels were with him that night and in the days that followed. Maybe angels are with all of us, much more than we realize

Grandma and I shared some endless moments together. One special day we drove to see her mother, my Great Grandma Scott. Jeanie Crawford Dickson Scott was a gentle lady with a strong Scottish brogue. Her once red hair now sparkled silver. We met for the first time in her humble and quiet home. Grandma Ann introduced us and instantly I loved her, but didn't know why. We were born in different centuries, almost 80 years apart. Yet something in her face reached deep into my heart.

It was a lovely day in Glasgow when Jeanie Crawford Dickson was born on August 10, 1879. John Scott began his life's journey with a small head start on June 9, 1877 also in Glasgow. They met in that land of a million memories on the high roads of Scotland. On March 6, 1903 they walked on together, stronger than ever. Jeanie and John Scott sailed with their two young children, Ann and John Jr, to America in 1906. Work was abundant there and good things were spoken about that great land of opportunity.

Jeanie was a petite yet strong lady. Many were surprised when their third child, Tom, was born tipping the baby scale at an amazing fifteen pounds. Now kinships run deep in Scotland. After a few years in America, Jeanie's heart yearned to see home. She and the kids sailed for Scotland in June of 1912, passing through the same iceberg fields where the Titanic had sunk just two months earlier. They returned for several happy seasons, but the outbreak of World War 1 kept them there even longer. They were finally scheduled to sail on a return voyage to America aboard the RMS Lusitania, but the great passenger ship never arrived. She was torpedoed and sunk on May 7, 1915 before reaching port. Jeanie and her three children had to wait almost an entire year before another voyage became possible. Jeanie Scott held firm during that and so many other voyages of life. She truly kept a brave Scottish heart.

Grandma Ann, Great Grandma Scott and I shared a lasting hug before we parted, not realizing we had just spanned four generations in a few brief moments. A couple years later, we all gathered to celebrate Grandma Scott's happy 90th birthday in Burbank. I was cheering for her to make 100 and she almost did. Jeanie set sail once more, this time for a beautiful and most welcome shore.

While there in California, Grandma was my favorite guide for a happy trip to Disneyland. A new attraction called Pirates of the Caribbean had recently opened and we both felt like becoming buccaneers for a day. Argh Grandma–walk the plank! After rescuing my companion from a certain swashbuckling fate, we sailed toward Frontierland and freedom. We pressed on through the deep jungles of Adventureland. Grandma was especially animated to hear the cheerful chorus of It's A Small World in Fantasyland. We chose two Tinkerbell figurines to bring home for mother and carefully wrapped them with love. By the time we reached Tomorrowland, I looked at the apple Grandma gave me. We could only imagine the future and I was getting hungry. Yet, one big chomp of my fresh apple and I was satisfied with a single mega byte. An orange sun began to set as a day at Disneyland was fully etched in our hearts. Grandma's home breathed a peaceful calm as we rested for the night. Tinkerbell must have touched us with a magic wand because we slept for a long time, even till new morning light.

Grandma invited me on another special quest as I accompanied her to Forest Lawn Memorial Park in Glendale. There on a dignified cemetery stone was her father and my Great Grandfather's name. John Scott lived a purposeful life, as we all do, in the moving mosaic of time. Not far away, Grandma led me to another memorial stone. The name Walt Disney glistened in the sun as I discovered it really was a small world after all.

Everything Grandma and Grandpa grew seemed to grow well. Deep red roses lined their narrow drive. Orange, avocado and lemon trees flourished in a small grove of Eden. Buckets of bright orange filled their kitchen where freshly squeezed juice flowed like a natural spring. I often watched a blanket of golden leaves gather beneath their citrus trees. Then Grandpa introduced me to his manual leaf catching mower and gladly demonstrated how to harvest the daily crop. Grandpa was a hard worker and even better manager. He enjoyed watching my activities from a soft patio lounge chair. I swept the yard with diligent precision and gathered an impressive mound of fallen leaves. Every leaf was similar yet each was unique. Summer leaves once soft and tender, now autumn jewels shown with splendor. Grandma and Grandpa had beautiful crops and some of their best were cherished grandkids.

It was time to go home now. I held Grandma and Grandpa as each gave a long goodbye. Perfect love seemed to flow through them as I felt again what forever should be. A peaceful palm gently waved in the Burbank breeze, just one more goodbye before we leave.

Going to see mother's folks in Texas was always a grand event. Alma and E. L.Wilson Jr., Mimi and Grandad as we affectionately called them, were ageless diamonds in our growing tapestry of life. They stood just this side of heaven and created cheerful pearls of love. You could easily mark the middle of your compass with Texas and from there proceed to many happy destinations. Now Dumas sat atop the Panhandle of Texas, somewhere between New York City and Los Angeles. Though not so large as Dallas, its noble spirit graced the plains. Mimi and Grandad still lived there as we first came to visit.

The drive from Las Vegas to Dumas seemed long, but there were fascinating points along the way. Route 66 was studded with stops that spoke real Americana. I was especially interested in those that offered a full supply of Big Hunk candy bars. Mimi and Grandad patiently awaited our arrival and we called from a pay phone in Amarillo to let them know we were almost there. The small porch light glowed warmly and a screen door opened widely as we pulled in. Everyone slept well that night as a Great Plains breeze filtered through their peaceful home. Mimi was up early the next morning and made a hearty breakfast for all. Grandad offered me ten cents to wash my hands before we began and I readily accepted. Everything about their 1960s kitchen seemed so modern.

Mimi, what was it like when you and Grandad were growing up?

Her eyes flickered like fire struck opals.

Well, Donnie boy, how much do you want to know?

She drew a deep and enduring breath.

Alma Lorene Johnson was born on Sunday, November 1, 1908 in Eastland County, Texas. She was third in a full basket of nine kids, two boys and seven precious girls. Her parents, Walter William Johnson and Mona Gabriella Dillard, began raising most of them in Eastland following their marriage of 1903 in Comanche, Texas. Alma was just eight when her family moved from Eastland to Collingsworth County in the Texas Panhandle. She often walked next to their covered wagons during the long journey. Alma's grandparents, Jefferson Roman Johnson and Mary Jane Lucinda Pearce, had also moved to Collingsworth County shortly before Walter and Mona's arrival. I guess the grass often does look greener on the other side of the hill … or prairie.

Jeff and Mary Johnson were married around New Year's Day 1876 in Lee County, Mississippi, about six months before General Custer took a wrong turn up at the Little Bighorn. Alma's maternal grandparents, Howard Burton Dillard and Sarah C. Hale, were also married around 1876 in Mississippi and took an early flight to Texas soon thereafter. Alma's great-grandparents, Marcus Alonzo Pearce and Patsy Ann Rachel Weaver, were married the day after Christmas 1850 in Itawamba County, Mississippi. Marc and his brothers served in the 5th Alabama Cavalry during the Civil War.

Patsy's younger brother, Robert Louis Shafer Weaver, enlisted early in the 1st Mississippi Infantry. He was captured in 1862 at Fort Donelson, Tennessee by troops of Ulysses S. Grant. Following a later exchange, R.L.S. continued to serve until taken again, this time at Port Hudson, Louisiana in 1863. Patsy's older brother, Calvin Dickson Weaver, joined the 43rd Mississippi Infantry. After serving through much of the War and just four months before it was over, he was seriously wounded at the Battle of Nashville in 1864. Calvin died in a civil war hospital on Christmas Day.

Alma's great-great-grandparents, John Madison Woods Pearce and Elizabeth Skinner, brought their family from Georgia to Alabama around 1848. J.M.W., Betsie and their seven boys embraced a new life among the rolling waters and fertile fields of Marion County. With determined muscle and strong sinew, Pearce's Mills flourished for 50 years in a Northwestern Alabama sun. Another pair of Alma's great-great-grandparents, Frederick Weaver and Rachel Young, originally hailed from South Carolina and Kentucky. They were married in October of 1829, almost a hundred years before Alma and E.L. tied the knot. Around 1870, they left the familiar surroundings of Itawamba County, Mississippi and joined a wagon train west to Texas. Many of the Johnson, Dillard, Pearce and Weaver families followed similar trails of promise. All of them led to Texas.

Mimi, your bacon and biscuits are really good.

Here, have some fried potatoes, she urged.

They're Wanda's favorite.

Now E.L.Wilson Jr. was born the day before Christmas, 1905 in the small town of Rule, Haskell County. He was the second of four boys and three strong girls. Elbert Lee Wilson and Tallulah Belle Raymond lifted seven stars in an epic panorama called Texas. E.L. Jr. labored much growing up on a family farm. Work was something you did before breakfast. His tall lanky frame became burnished in the kiln of a steady Panhandle sun. Cotton was an ever-present resilient crop in Collingsworth County and E.L. picked enough of it to wrap the moon twice. Attending church and school in the Salt Fork Community brought good balance to E.L. during his youth. Tallulah adored and often called him, " my little man."

Alma was ten when she and E.L. first met. By the age of fifteen, her heart saw only him. Alma was almost seventeen, when she and E.L. were happily married on October 7, 1925 in Wellington, Texas. On their honeymoon, they celebrated by picking cotton. E.L. would later write a special letter to Alma and it began like this:

In nineteen hundred and twenty-five, I married the sweetest little girl alive…

Well, together they raised three lovely girls – Margie Louise, Wanda Nell and Wilma Janell at a small farmhouse of simple means. Everyone could see they sure did raise em pretty in Texas. Atwell E. Barnhart sure did as he married and swept Margie away. Wanda journeyed west where William J. Brady offered her his heart. Harold R. Green first met Wilma as each strolled through a tomato patch. They soon fell in love and never looked back.

Mimi, the fried taters are yummy!

Here, have some scrambled eggs too.

Raymond L. Wilson, E.L.'s brother, brought smiles everywhere he went, even as school principal in Happy, Texas.

Did you know that Raymond was named after Tallulah Belle's dad, Francis Newton Raymond? Grandaddy Raymond was born a way back in 1849 at Rochester, New York. Francis left home at age sixteen and came west to Colorado. He worked in the gold mines for a time, then moved on to Texas. Francis served as first lieutenant in the Wise County Texas Rangers for a brief season. His marriage to Martha Jane Start in 1874 at Weatherford drew him away from that service and brought a career change for the better. Marriage can do that you know. Francis and Mattie Raymond raised a full crop of seven kids, two boys and five girls. For some reason, girls seem to grow well in Texas.

The Raymonds lived and owned land in several Texas counties. At Rising Star in Eastland County, they ran a successful country store. In Moran, Shackelford County they did the same and bought more open land. At Old Ochiltree, which became Perryton up the Panhandle way, Francis acquired several sections of land from the railroad for $1 an acre in 1901. Francis and Martha Raymond had considerable property, but their real wealth was in the heart and the lasting friendship they freely gave to others. Daughter Lula Belle married Elbert Lee Wilson on November 1, 1899 in Albany, Texas. A new century was about to begin and the west had already been won. The 1900's seemed so futuristic.

Elbert Lee Wilson was born September 8, 1874 in Fayette County, Tennessee. One thing was certain, he quickly became a Texas original. Elbert was seen at least once plowing his fields in a dress. Perhaps, he was just trying to dress for success. While staying with relatives on a rather calm New Year's Eve, Elbert waited till midnight. Suddenly, he led some young 'uns on a charge through the house, banging pie and cake pans together. Everyone was so startled, they thought the Civil War had started all over again.

Now Elbert grew from a large family of eighteen kids, he being plumb in the middle. I guess John M. Wilson and Catherine Josephine Zellner had a good relationship at their farm in Hickory Withe, Tennessee. C.J., or Josie as she was often called, was a devoted mother and affectionate wife. Josie and John were married in August of 1861 at Hickory Withe, two weeks before her sixteenth birthday. A month or so later, Josie's new husband enlisted in the 38th Tennessee Infantry. John held Josie once more as they gave a heartfelt goodbye. After serving almost a year, John's health was fading. He was discharged in 1862 and came home to Josie.

Josie's close brother, John William Zellner, enlisted at the age of seventeen in the lucky 13th Tennessee Infantry. He was seriously wounded at the Battle of Shiloh in April of 1862. John was then wounded and captured at Richmond, Kentucky in August of '62. Following his exchange at City Point, Virginia in May of 1863, John saw action at Chickamauga and was wounded again. J.W. Zellner tried to hold a line at New Hope Church, Georgia in 1864, but was struck again. He struggled at the Battle of Atlanta in May of '64 and was wounded once more. John W. Zellner and the 13th Tennessee were surrendered and paroled on May 2, 1865 at Greensboro, North Carolina. If promotions were given each time a soldier was wounded, Sgt Zellner could have been a General. John married a sweet girl, Jane Anderson Cherry, after his first wife, Willie E. Patton, passed on. And by George, those Pattons … well, that's another story.

Josie's folks, Marion Zellner and Martha Adeline Alexander, were married in February of 1842 in Hernando, Desoto, Mississippi. I'm sure Marion said a prayer or two when he later served as Chaplain of Green's 12th Tennessee Cavalry. Now Marion's grandad, George Peter Zellner, was himself a British soldier during the Revolution. It seems like someone's always a feudin with somebody else. Martha Adeline saw almost a hundred years, just four months shy. She carried on from 1820 to 1920 and knew folks from the American Revolution, War of 1812, Civil War and World War 1. I think she was tired of all those wars and just wanted to go home.

Martha's great-great-grandad, Hezekiah Alexander, was a signer of The Mecklenburg Declaration of Independence on May 20, 1775 in North Carolina. Their old rock house in Charlotte is just as strong today as when they built it in 1774. Hez's brother, John McKnitt Alexander, was secretary of that convention and a signer too. Now Thomas Jefferson later wrote a letter to John Adams mentioning John McKnitt and a timeline of remembered events. There seemed to be some question as to which declaration was actually first, The Mecklenburg Declaration of May 20, 1775 or the nationally recognized Declaration of July 4, 1776. Maybe they were both first in their own way. All I know is we told those British to get on home. Everyone felt better when that war was over and celebrations went on for months. Hezekiah's lovely daughters were soon invited to a special party honoring General Washington.

Well, I guess that's about it.

Donnie, would you like some more eggs?

Breakfast was mighty good, Mimi.

Thank you, but I'm full.

Mimi, I have another question.

Good, we can talk a little more over lunch.

A Cornucopia Of Critters

Living in a desert or rainforest is almost the same, one has more trees and the other less rain. The critters we find there are happy at home among tropical leaves or dry desert stones. Our desert panorama quickly came alive as each new critter joyously arrived. Mother planted bright petunias all around the yard and they flourished with tender care. Resident chipmunks soon discovered just how tasty petunia petals could be and frequently scampered in for a flowerbed brunch. Now Phyllis was the first to spot an owl above our cypress tree. I saw the stately bird perched atop an eave as if searching a gourmet menu. Maybe owls are good luck. I guess it depends upon whose eyes you're looking through. A cautious chipmunk may see prime danger, but a patient owl sees prime rib.

A spry roadrunner sometimes appeared at our desert oasis and may have land surfed all the way in from Phoenix. The agile bird had a real crop of hair on its head and looked a bit like Rod Stewart. The nimble chaparral bird always seemed alert. One toasty day, a swift zebra-tailed lizard sprinted across the yard, closely followed by an excited roadrunner. At first, they appeared to be playing a friendly game of tag. Then I realized the roadrunner was looking for lunch and was about to tell the zebra lizard – You're It!

A variety of wandering lizards found favor in our backyard paradise. I watched in wonder as these all-terrain climbers scaled granite like cinder block walls. Each day, they ascended and conquered their own El Capitans. Once they reached the capstone summit, a panoramic view of all things desert lay before them. I was drawn to these sage lizards and engaged one of them eye to eye, then looked deep into his soul. You see, I had been watching a new tv show called Star Trek and was now familiar with the process of thought transfer and mind-melding. First, I communicated to my terrestrial friend that I had no desire to eat him. I had already consumed two bowls of Lucky Charms for breakfast. As we became more acclimated and at ease with one another, mutual concerns were explored.

Is global warming real?

Yes, and he's quite comfortable with it.

Are there sufficient food resources?

Yes, ants and aphids are plentiful.

Is man encroaching upon natural habitat?

Yes, and he should stop digging up my burrows.

Is world peace possible?

Yes, if hawks and roadrunners stop trying to eat me.

We shared many insights during an enlightening visit before bidding each other a fond farewell. Live long and prosper my earthly friend.

A large lime green mantis often kept vigil near our patio door. Whenever a hapless bug wandered by, his prayers were speedily answered. An impressive daddy longlegs frequently danced across that porch like Fred Astaire. I just can't recall if he and the praying mantis ever got together for lunch. We also had a few flying June bugs in the yard. When airborne, the metallic green beetles sounded like an approaching squadron of B-17 Flying Fortresses. I courageously ran in every direction away from them. Occasionally, giant green grasshoppers appeared on our guest list of curious critters. The goliath grasshoppers may have come from a distant rainforest forgotten by time. Perhaps, they escaped from a nonexistent experiment at nearby Area 51.

Dragonflies in the desert are beautiful to behold, as they would be anywhere. Their brilliant blue, glistening green and rich red colors could brighten any day. We watched as these fantastic fliers landed gracefully and balanced motionless on single blades of grass. In gymnastics they would have received a perfect ten. Surprisingly, some landed upon my arm and were content to rest there. I wonder if those gentle dragonflies, like people, realized just how beautiful they really were.

My melody of desert life swirled in the sand, where heroic sungold horny toads made a mighty stand. I watched in admiration as a hungry horny toad with his regal crown, stood majestically, like Lady Liberty, upon the sunswept ground. Stalwartly standing by a red wooden gate, near an entrance to our desert isle, I heard him sincerely say, Give me your tired, poor sunburnt ants, send them all my way! For him, every day was an all you could eat ant buffet.

Our horny toad watchdog had ruby-red designs along his rough sandstone back. He seemed to blend with the color of our barn door gate and red brick patio. He and I soon became brothers of drifting sand and desert sun.

Early one morning I walked by the pool, ready to skim any bugs or leaves that floated therein. To my great sadness, I saw the shape of a large horny toad lying upside down on the pool bottom. I quickly stretched forth the long-handled skimmer net and carefully raised a lifeless form to the surface.

Could this be my favorite horny toad?

There on his back were streaming red rays like a living sunset. My heart was broken and I began to cry.

Please God, don't let my horny toad die.

You can bring anything back to life.

You brought Lazarus back from the dead.

Please bring my horny toad back to life.

You can do it, I cried.

Suddenly, I remembered how people could be revived by giving them something called CPR. My horny toad had no respiration, movement or sign of life. He just lay there on the stone-grey kool deck. Maybe horny toad CPR could help bring him back to life. I quickly wiped aside my tears as he lay motionless upon his back. I placed two fingers upon his pure white chest and gently began to press. Several times I pressed, keep trying – again. Nothing happened.

God, send life back into my horny toad.

He can live forever if You make him alive again.

More CPR … then some frothy foam bubbled from his mouth.

Can it be?

Almost every gentle push now brought forth more water.

Then a small twitch.

I eased him right-side up and within a few moments an eye began to open.

This was a miracle.

God had answered my pleas and I knew it. Gradually, the once lifeless horny toad began to move and again I said Thank You.

I was reminded at seven years of age, while kneeling beside a backyard pool, that God really does care and hears everyone's heartfelt prayers. The horny toad and I were both reborn that day.

Summer showers can bring forth abundant life in a southwestern desert. Mother and I watched as a skyward scroll quickly unfurled. Cumulus clouds began to billow, filling the heat soaked horizon. Gentle rumbles began to roll as thick laden clouds drew near. Quiet crackles rippled through the air as ionic excitement lit up the atmosphere. Now mother didn't like thunderstorms and would often moan while covering her ears. She had a favorite dog while growing up, a collie named Old Pal. Whenever a storm rolled in, Old Pal would lead a retreat under the nearest bed and not come out till sunny skies prevailed. Mother and Old Pal seemed to have attended the same survival school. As thunder heralded a coming storm, mother headed for a bedroom bunker. We all loved the rain, mother just preferred it without thunder. Sometimes it didn't come that way on life's menu.

An ever thirsty desert slurped the summer rain. Every living thing, chiefly creosote, offered up fragrant aromas in thanksgiving as joyful birds proclaimed new songs of celebration. An endless network of puddles appeared and could remain for days. Flotillas of drifting dragonflies found happy home in this brief land of a thousand lakes. Newborn horny toads and tiny lizards began to emerge. Quiet brittlebush and desert mallow burst forth in sungold yellow and luscious orange. Summer rain, with or without thunder, was the tofu of life, bringing forth flavor from everything it met.

Our eyes were lifted and cares lightened the day bluebirds suddenly appeared.

Donnie, come quickly and see the beautiful bluebirds, mother excitedly said.

Look at how many there are!

Phyllis also witnessed the rare and vivid event.

Our eyes beheld a sea of approaching blue as it fluttered from above. As if invitations were given and gladly received, the air around us filled with rapture. Each arriving guest wore the finest tuxedo of bonnie blue to the festive gathering. There among our garnished pyracantha, the great host of happy bluebirds enjoyed a banquet of bright red berries. They stayed just long enough to thrill our senses with their wonderful presence. We hoped the cheerful birds would soon return and one day they did.

Where did all those beautiful bluebirds go?

I think they truly found the top of a rainbow.

As twilight glowed in a western sky, some critters danced in the desert night. Phyllis, Linda and I also set forth on several evening safaris. Geckos were a special sight and most welcome in our desert pavilion. The banded geckos with large heads, translucent skin and thick tails appeared otherworldly. Occasionally, we'd find one or two enjoying an evening swim at the pool. When gently held, they made an unusual squeaking sound which I believe may have been code talk among gecko scouts.

A deep satin sky enveloped our tranquil desert night as we sat in the evening air. Linda ventured barefoot through backyard grass, unaware of the piercing danger that lay so near. Something bit me, she woefully cried. Searching with flashlights, we found a supersize scorpion. Linda's foot was quickly treated the old-fashioned way to remove venom. The defiant scorpion, still arching its tail, was fully prepared to strike again. A well made boot with authority from above brought a crushing end to the conflict. A peaceful calm eventually returned to our desert canopy and the timeless wonders of night.

A desert tarantula briefly roamed our backyard bonanza of bugs. He seemed shy, somewhat reserved and didn't bark much. We held several observational meetings and discussed specific matters of ecological importance. As we voted upon key issues, the conservative tarantula gently raised an arm four or five times. I reminded my fuzzy friend that only one vote per resident creature was allowed. It was then that I realized our oft voting visitor may have been a career politician. Though always welcome, he apparently moved on to another desert district.

The open desert west of our family home was like a swatch of Wyoming wilderness. As a young boy, I often explored an expansive frontier of wild mesquite and desert dunes.

Mother, I'm ready to hike in the desert today.

Take plenty of water and don't go too far, she said.

The canteen is full, I assured her, while lifting it from the fridge.

Mother was the best outfitter, supplying tangy mustard and salami sandwiches along with vital coconut cookies. My large canvas backpack was like a faithful mule, but I had to do all the pulling.

When will you be back? she asked.

Probably around sundown.

Ok Donnie, but watch for snakes, they like to come out about that time.

I was well prepared and carried a cub scout knife, flashlight, cookies, crackers and other essential items in case I met a bear or became marooned.

The Mohave sun was set extra high that day and the desert simmered on soft broil. The ice cubes placed in my canteen had long since surrendered but still tasted refreshingly sweet. Water is so essential that some folks name their towns after it. There's Sweetwater, Stillwater, Clearwater, even a place called Badwater. I guess everyone needs some good water.

Well, I saw several lizards, a couple chipmunks, a whole herd of grasshoppers and even a desert iguana on my journey. Coming back, I decided to stop by an overgrown mesquite bush and rest in some shade. Evidently, someone else had the same cool idea. There on the soft shady sand appeared a long rope wrapped in perfect circles. It looked like the top of a carefully woven basket with attractive designs. My mind wasn't sure of what my eyes were seeing. Upon closer inspection, I realized it was a large sidewinder rattlesnake. I looked closely at the heart-shaped head. Its eyes were closed and the rattler appeared to be resting. I curiously gazed upon what seemed to be horns raised above each eye. The snake's head was alluring and its colors enticing. The pit viper could instantly have struck my face, but somehow didn't sense my presence. Perhaps, an unseen angel kept the sidewinder sleeping till a curious lad was headed home.

Dad had told me about sidewinders and other desert snakes. Colorful coral snakes were always a danger, but noble kingsnakes were forever good. I found a recently run over kingsnake by the side of our road. The black and white bands it bore were magnificent. In admiration, I brought it home for everyone to see. For some reason, mother didn't want me to bring dead snakes home. So, I parted with the retired reptile and gave it an honorable burial, one befitting a noble kingsnake. Mother seemed especially pleased with my thoughtful decision.

An early morning sun streaked across the waking sky as mother stood near an expansive picture window. Every new day brought a kaleidoscope of changing colors upon our desert canvas of life. Her alexandrite eyes sparkled as she celebrated this new day. Out of the vista a new critter appeared, trotting towards the front planter box. Stalwart ears and bushy tail, why jumpin cactus – it's a fox. The curious fellow explored our flagstone porch, then sat in perfect triumph. He and mother gazed through the glass admiring one another. Many of the resident chipmunks were unusually quiet that day. Mother thought of offering the friendly fox some Little Friskies before he ventured on the way. I guess every last creature of sand and of space, seeks for a harbor to call his own place. Critters came and sometimes stayed, almost all were welcome in those rich desert days.

Our cornucopia of critters wouldn't be complete without a few cats. Tini was a brave Russian Blue who came to us as a nomad in the night. Her sleek grey coat, embraced by moonlight, emerged from the desert darkness. A soft meow was answered with an open door and joyful hearts. She soon became a loyal friend watching over our home and us too. Dad called her a real mouser and Tini reigned as lioness over a vast savanna.

The desert with all its stark beauty can also be a rough place. One morning, Tini lay quiet on an outdoor deck. She didn't look so well and also wouldn't eat. Upon closer inspection, we noticed two small puncture wounds above her eye. Tini had been bitten by a snake. Time would tell if she was strong enough to survive. I gently touched her weakened body and expressed how much we loved her. Hold on Tini, you're going to make it. Every few hours, we checked on our devoted friend and wondered if she could pull through. After five days, she began to eat a little and eventually did get better. Everyone was glad to see her up and roaming again.

A few months later, Tini was eating more and doing better than ever. We then noticed a rather large protruding belly. Mother announced that Tini was going to have kittens. Phyllis, Linda and I prepared some warm blankets and a special bed for her in the garage. As the time of Tini's delivery drew near, we comforted and stayed by her side. We watched in wonder as two snow white kittens appeared. She carefully groomed and nuzzled each of the fragile new cubs. To our surprise, she then birthed a third which was satin black as the sacred night. Mother and dad said there were now three new kittens for three great kids. Phyllis and Linda chose the first two, naming them Taffy and Tuffy. I was drawn to the special one wrapped in midnight black.

What will you name your kitten? mother asked.

I thought for a magical moment, then called him Spooky.

Yes, that's a really good name, she smiled.

But he needs a full legal name, I added.

His full name shall be Herman Jay Spooky, I proclaimed.

He can carry my middle name with honor.

Mother and dad smiled again, nodding with approval.

We kept a caring eye on Tini and her three tiny kittens. A few days later, the kitchen to garage door was open and Tini entered carrying one of the kittens in her mouth. She carefully looked each way while transporting her little one through the house. Ultimately, she entered my room and maneuvered behind an old dresser. There she somehow deposited the little critter in a drawer of socks and soft T-shirts. She soon returned with each of the other protesting youngsters and hid them in like manner. For several weeks, I had three new and sometimes noisy roommates.

Our kittens quickly grew as they and all of us learned more about life. Spooky became a close member of my Hot Wheels inner circle and racing team. He eagerly chased every live car as it sped along the orange oval track. That season we all held a favorite cat for a brief Christmas photo. More paws meant more fun, but our growing critter family wasn't yet done. A few months later, another hopeful cat with lots of love to give, wandered into our welcome home and happy hearts to live. It was Easter and we named our new cat Peter. Now I didn't have a brother, but Peter and I became close, perhaps as brothers could be. There were only so many moments in life and some of the best were of Peter and me.

Our travels through sunswept vistas sometimes brought a joyous surprise.

Look mother, there's a turtle! Can we bring it home?

She slowed the steadfast Chevy truck as I welcomed a new passenger aboard. Each desert tortoise that we embraced found pleasant pasture in our sandy yard. These humble herbivores received tender turtle care and a generous supply of iceberg lettuce. The first member of our turtle family had a small gold patch that someone had previously painted on its back. "Goldie" was a true pioneer and blazed new desert trails for other brave tortoises to follow. Another turtle we found had three small sections of its shell that had once been painted in a spectrum of bright colors. Rainbow liked to run and dig deep burrows in the yard. GoGo and GiGi were younger turtles and spent some time by the pool. Then there was Tiny, a really small tortoise you could easily hold in one hand. We had a special place for him on the patio where he received extra care. Tiny sometimes went with me for supervised romps through lush garden foliage.

Some family friends were going on vacation and asked if we could turtle sit for their special tortoise. We agreed and were met by one of the largest turtles this side of Texas. It looked like a living brontosaurus but was gentle and kind. I introduced Tiny to the mighty matriarch as they gazed upon each other with admiration. One morning, mother set Tiny and his cardboard box near the backyard well. Later, she came back crying and we asked what had happened.

I fried Tiny, she sorrowfully said.

I thought he needed some sun and forgot to bring him back under the patio shade.

I'm so sorry, she cried.

It's ok, it was just an accident, I said.

I reached toward mother and held her for a long time.

Tiny's in turtle heaven now, it's alright, I whispered.

Amid our turtle tragedy, we still created unique moments of fun in those early desert days. I had watched the Kentucky Derby on tv and proposed we all gather for a great tortoise race. Mother cranked the Kodak movie camera to film the epic event. Phyllis, Linda and I each chose a trusted turtle, one that could carry us triumphantly at the El Camino Downs. This was a run for the roses with the winning tortoise to be crowned with creosote and great honor. Linda's turtle looked doubtful and Phyllis wrestled with her tepid tortoise. My sure steed had the look of a champion and was already chomping at lettuce, ready to run. We placed our favorites on the circular drive starting line. Mother gave the awaited signal – Go!

And they're off!

Linda leapt skyward, unleashing incredible jumping jacks, urging her tortoise on. Phyllis counselled her tentative turtle to press forward with all haste. I wisely held some crisp lettuce before my desert dynamo, but he had already become somewhat full at the starting line. It was close for several thrilling moments. Linda's turtle then turned in confusion and wandered towards a distant mirage. Phyllis folded her arms as her tortoise seemed to stall. I carefully instructed my galloping galapago to engage the turtle turbo, but he too began to waver. No turtle raced more swiftly or valiantly as mine did that day. Indeed, if I had run a mile in his shell, could I have done so well?

The time soon came that we released our courageous turtles back to the desert wild. I gave each an Irish blessing and let them run free. Still, as a southwestern sun begins to set, I turn my head to hear, a distant and familiar call, of fearless turtles standing tall, a call of the desert wild.

Age Of Discovery

My third grade year was a wonderful time of renaissance and reflection. Mrs. Lang was always an angel and also a favorite teacher. Here we learned the flowing art of cursive handwriting. The practice and style of each letter became a beautiful form of written communication. I began to feel personal pride in my penmanship abilities and graceful signature. Our teacher also encouraged us to write an original poem in class. After much thought, Myrtle the Turtle came to be. May I share it with you here.

Myrtle the Turtle

There once was a very shy turtle,

Her name was meek little Myrtle,

She entered a track race,

But couldn't keep a fast pace

And ended up loosing her girdle.

This poem may be one of the greatest literary works of our time. Mrs. Lang just had a way of bringing forth the best in us.

Along with writing, my eight-year old smile was simply outstanding. A few kids even honored me with the noble nickname of Buck Teeth. Now this wasn't due to the prominence of my two front teeth. It was because I didn't have any. In fact, all four of my upper front teeth had been missing since early childhood. Our first dentist declared that my four front baby teeth lacked sufficient enamel. He recommended their immediate removal and the formation of a small denture. Now I don't recall ever agreeing to this. At just one year of age, I faced a dental dilemma. After several decades and the dawn of a new millennium, my faith in gentle dentistry has somewhat been restored. During those younger years, an occasional request was made.

Please God, help me grow some new front teeth.

Well, one glorious day upon the school playground, I noticed a strange surprise. Something solid was poking through my empty gumline. I gently examined the object with my tongue and wondered if my seven-year dental drought was now over. I was careful not to touch the emerging tooth too much, so it wouldn't get pressed back inside my gums. After school, I excitedly reported to mother my new discovery. She looked and confirmed that indeed, my time of toothless delivery had come. For days, I awoke to see if my new tooth was still there. Eventually, all four of my front teeth gleamed anew.

How many things could I do with my new front teeth?

Every large apple now feared me. Thick juicy steaks trembled before my gaping mouth. Somehow, I humbly decided to be patient and take everything just one bite at a time.

Becoming a Cub Scout at eight years of age opened a new door of exciting activity. Mother and I both thought the navy blue uniform was a great fit. Everything from the cub scout cap and crisply folded neckerchief to the hallmarked shirt, trousers and blue belt with brass buckle, all brought an elevated sense of duty and honor. Mother helped me really look good, sharp enough to have ridden with the U.S. Cavalry. I wore the new Bobcat pin with pride and often thought of the challenge to do a good turn daily. Achieving the ranks of Wolf and Bear, each with silver arrowheads, brought feelings of great accomplishment. Mother cheerfully volunteered for Cub Scout events and was asked to serve as den mother, which she gladly did. We sometimes gathered for great adventure in unique places. At a nearby farm, we met some handsome ostriches that were taller than any of us. One young cub, Elliot, got so excited by his close encounter with the giant birds, that he just had to phone home.

Halloween was always a sweet time of year and our cub scout pack announced an enchanted evening of activities for all. The spooky event included a costume contest where parents were invited to help their cubs create a fun and memorable outfit. Dad had a scary good idea and began forming a custom stovepipe hat which he then painted in the darkest black. He applied an unusual mixture of mother's makeup to my once cherub like face. What resulted scared even the angels of grace. I cloaked myself with mother's old robe and wore her winter boots. In my heart, I felt the real possibility of being named Best in Show.

Many of the kids didn't recognize me and I thoroughly scared a couple parents whose child came dressed as Peter Pan. Well, the winning costume design was announced and my name echoed through the festive hall. I was called forward to receive a special prize and wondered what it might be. Was it a board game or maybe even a new bike? The pack leader offered congratulations, then handed me a new toothbrush. I sincerely thanked her but inwardly was a little disappointed. Yet, it was the fun of it all and nice thought that counted. Many of us then bobbed for apples in a large tub of water. Mother's mascara began to dribble and quickly run as I chased the elusive fruit.

I realized my mouth wasn't quite large enough to capture the oversized apples. This would easily remedy itself in just a few short years. I was glad to get home that night and begin a welcome process of facial restoration. Following a full jar of Noxema and several washcloths, I recognized myself once more.

When the Cub Scout Pinewood Derby rolled around, dad was eager to help design and craft a champion racer. We stared at the plain block of pinewood and four plastic wheels, imagining what it could become. Out came dad's famous yellow pad of paper, #3 pencil and most importantly, a generous bowl of popcorn from which to draw inspiration. What emerged on paper was an aerodynamic futuristic jet car, far surpassing anything Henry Ford could have envisioned. Excitement grew daily as we cut, trimmed and sanded our sleek machine. It now looked like an Indy car with twin turbos and dual exhaust. We gently lubricated each nail axle with graphite, all legal of course. What dazzling color should we paint it? Glistening gold was the unanimous choice.

We arrived at the derby event with our golden jet car in tow. Several downhill racing lanes had been erected, similar to alpine ski runs. Flat straightaways then stretched toward the ultimate finish line. We glanced at some of the other derby cars and couldn't help but feel a little proud of our own. Providence smiled and we did well in almost every racing heat. Then I noticed David, a tall and lanky scout, whose car seemed to easily win every preliminary race it ran. It looked like a jalopy but ran like a jaguar. Destiny would find us together in the derby finals. Our golden star sat alongside his surprising speedster. I was already happy, yet somehow knew it would take every bit of tailwind to carry a photo finish. We raced and cheered in a spirit of fun competition. I congratulated David when his car finished first. I felt pretty good with a second place ribbon, while the car dad designed was easily first in compliments. Perhaps, the special bonds of friendship among kids and their parents received the best blue ribbons of all.

As a Cub Scout, I gladly volunteered for the annual fundraising event of selling tickets to the Scout Fair. Mother let me stand in my nifty uniform by an entrance to Vegas Village and Wonder World while she did some grocery shopping. Some days I sold two, three or even four tickets to the upcoming fair. It felt good to contribute and mother shared in the positive experience. The first Scout Fair I attended was at the Las Vegas Convention Center. A vast sea of scouts seemed to flow in every direction. I happened to walk by an open door, and there were many, where two leaders asked if I could help make an important announcement. They gave me a large paper to read from and an even larger microphone.

Can you do it? they confidently asked.

Yes sir, I quickly saluted.

They introduced me over a live system as I officially opened and welcomed everyone to the 1969 Las Vegas Scout Fair. Later, I told mother of the exciting invitation and small part I played in the grand event.

Today, I hold a bronze Bobcat pin and carefully folded neckerchief in faded hands. What I really see are enduring emblems of a mother and dad's lasting love for me.

Our family living room sometimes became a glowing realm of wonder. Dad's keen mind was always imbued with fluorescent knowledge. His firm grasp of geologic science was truly tectonic. One of our favorite demonstrations was that of his ultraviolet light and phosphorescent rocks. Mother, Phyllis, Linda and I all gathered round as the colorful show began. His weathered hands held a variety of rock and mineral samples that soon sparkled. Dad knew the names of each stone as if they were beloved children. He invited us to hold each magical mineral near a bright light. Dad then produced his enchanting ultraviolet wand. As visible light faded, his black light wonder revealed the hidden beauties of each special stone. Calcite fluoresced a heavenly blue and fluorite a vivid violet. Willemite was a phosphorescent jewel of neon green, orange and blue. Every small stone or rough rock shone as a star in my hand. I wanted to behold their beauty forever. Eventually, our living room lights came back on and the joyous colors quickly dimmed. Some say we each radiate an exquisite aura unseen by natural eyes. I wonder if there's a special light that can help us to see the incredible beauties within.

I discovered at an early age that girls liked dolls and dainty homes. I embraced dinosaurs and rugged geologic stones. Perhaps I felt a kinship with those prehistoric kings. Maybe work as a dinosaur veterinarian lurked in some future offerings. My appetite for Jurassic cuisine became voracious as I devoured every dinosaur seen. Mother quickly realized I became engorged at every meal with Mesozoic meatloaf and trilobite souffle. Even dad was impressed with my Precambrian IQ. I began to sketch living dinosaur landscapes and was often carried away by curious raptors. Mother gave me a few extra jobs where I could earn a little money and I wisely invested in prehistoric figures. Earth tone models of thundering reptiles soon populated and rumbled through my room. Brontosaurus, Triceratops, Stegosaurus and Tyrannosaurus were just a few. Fortunately, they were mostly quiet at night so everyone could sleep.

I frequently ventured through untouched rifts of desert terrain searching for small marine fossils. A variety of surface rocks near our home also displayed the remains of tiny sea creatures suspended in time.

Donnie, what did you find today?

Here's a grey rock with 17 small fossils.

Isn't it pretty?

Yes it is, mother smiled.

I also gathered flakes of glass like obsidian and red jasper spread along the desert floor. My favorite find was a round fossil type rock that naturally separated through the center. The ancient fossil looked like an egg with a delicate embryo inside.

Dad and I occasionally drove a highway towards California in search of quality building sand. We travelled as Admiral Byrd along winding and forgotten roads as sunworn shovels jockeyed for position in the old pickup truck. Dad rotated his head as a manual compass, scanning the dry horizon.

There it is! he firmly pointed. Just where I remembered it would be.

Together we hoisted fully laden shovels of exquisite native sand. Our hungry truck welcomed the newfound feast and was filled to satisfaction. While loading the truck, I noticed a glittering rock formation. I hefted a large crystalline portion and offered it to dad.

That's a pretty hunk of calcite, real nice, he affirmed.

A natural group of crystals were arrayed in spectacular fashion as prismatic light danced upon the trillion shaped surface. We gladly kept and admired it for many years.

Dad and I shared a rich world of geologic rocks and minerals. For us, a deep purple amethyst was worthy of a king's crown. Rose quartz could easily grace a queen's scepter or hem of her royal gown. Each day of life is a precious stone as we gather them in and build our home.

Mother and dad always tried to give us a few nice presents at Christmas and truly were good parents all year round. One holiday season, Phyllis and Linda got new roller skates. I was surprised to receive a large pogo stick.

What is it and what does it do? I asked.

It's a pogo stick, Donnie.

What can you do with it? I wondered aloud.

You jump up and down on it, dad explained.

I observed two foot supports, a round pole housed within an industrial size spring and handlebars near the top.

Donnie, just pogo outside and not in the house, mother said with a pleasant yet concerned look.

I tried to mount up but fell off a few times. It was like trying to ride a one-legged horse while jumping up and down. I soon pogoed around the circular drive. I pogoed in the neighbor's yard and down the street. Each upward lift gave me a better view of the world and also provided thorough digestion. Perhaps I should have purchased pogo insurance. Yet, if the pogo premiums and deductibles were too high and exclusions too extensive, it may not have panned out anyway. I continued forward and bounded toward a friend's house.

Hi Sam, want to try my new pogo stick?

Sure, Donzo.

He swiftly launched himself into the air, but Sam and the pogo stick landed in different locations.

You've got to hold on, I reminded him.

Then our grandparents came for a visit.

Grandma, would you like to pogo?

Oh, not today honey.

Well, if you change your mind, I can show you how to do it.

My dependable pogo also had a built-in counter. I remember the first time I made it to 68 jumps without crashing, then 100. One incredible day, I eclipsed 700 consecutive jumps. It was like breaking the sound barrier. Such pogo potential could really take me places. Why, I could have jumped all the way to Vermont. You see, a young boy with boundless energy and a pogo present from loving parents – some gifts truly are exponential.

As a young lad, rubber frogs, snakes and spiders were abundantly available in most stores. The opportunity of strategically placing a lifelike frog or snake along my sisters path was well worth the one dollar investment. Their genuine surprise and precious response was simply delightful. Over time, finding fresh hiding places for the floppy snake became more of a challenge. With great hope, I placed it among some food items in the fridge. This resulted in my parents calling a powwow where it was determined that I was banned from all future frog and snake placements around the house, to which I reluctantly agreed. Well, a couple weeks later, dad was in the garage and found another rubber snake on the ground.

Donnie did it again, he moaned.

As dad reached to pick up the perfect decoy, he was startled to see it move. This was not a rubber snake, but the real McCoy!

Well, I've since decided to quit scaring my sisters and by the age of 36 had stopped completely.

Fourth grade was a time of great decision, a time for stepping up to the plate. Tryouts for the school softball team were boldly announced with major league potential on deck. Perhaps this was a path I should pursue in life. This could be a golden step up towards overcoming my frequent kickball catastrophes. Most team captains usually chose me as a late round draft pick for every playground squad. The one miraculous exception occurred when my friend Kurt chose me third during a glorious selection process. I suddenly wore an invisible Superman cape and sent the rusty red kickball sailing over centerfield. The airborne ball and my esteem soared skyward. Now here was a softball diamond set in fields of emerald green. Something knocked at my small trellis window and I opened to find a new sports dream.

Tryouts began promptly after school and I added my name to a lengthy list of hopeful stars. A coach called me to the plate and I stepped forward into the unknown. My first taste of glory was a sweet strike. The second softball pitch drifted toward the plate as an elusive UFO, then vanished before a mighty swing. Strike Two. First impressions were important and the third pitch could determine if I was a rising Babe Ruth star or a melted Baby Ruth bar. I carefully calculated incoming velocity and prevailing wind speed. My nine year old eyes bore down on the planetary size softball. A tremendous rush of wind was felt as the Planet X softball passed over my earthbound bat. Strike Three. It was like trying to hit a flying potato. My first plate appearance drew murmurs from the crowd. Time for a switch to the outfield. Coach placed me so far out, I could almost count satellites in orbit. I stood in a lonely part of the field where there wasn't much action. Then someone smashed a stratospheric shot toward my remote location.

Please God, help me catch this ball.

I maneuvered left, then back, further back. The meteoric ball descended through a light blue atmosphere as it plunged toward earth. My arms felt like iron pegs as I braced for impact. Many eyes were upon me as the spherical miracle embedded itself in my glove.

He caught it! someone yelled.

Indeed, and I quickly thanked heaven for a moment of redemption. I hadn't hit the ball but was a momentary star for catching one.

The following tryout session found me yet again at the furthest point of centerfield civilization. Remarkably, another long ball was lifted toward my territory and again I called upon heaven to stretch forth a helping hand. Somehow, I pulled down another hpme run ball and triumphantly jogged through a welcoming infield.

Nice catch, coach acknowledged.

Can I be on the team? I humbly asked.

You're on it, he quickly agreed.

As mother picked me up from school that day, I eagerly shared the good news.

Mother, I made the team – I made it!

That's wonderful, she smiled.

There are many great sports in which to participate, but I found this to be one where catching flies was actually good for you.

When our flagship elementary school announced the opportunity to participate in an American history stage presentation, I decided to join the merry crew. A charming lady visited our fourth grade class and asked who would be interested in playing a part. She began to name key characters who played pivotal roles during our nation's star-studded history. Several students lifted their arms as exciting roles were delegated. When the courageous name of Davy Crockett was read, I found myself a ready volunteer. I had watched Fess Parker play a larger than life Crockett on tv and mother had already given me a Davy Crockett hat, so I looked the part.

You'll be fine, the director heartily agreed.

Can I carry my BB gun rifle on stage?

I don't see why not, the director nodded.

Then the part of Abraham Lincoln was offered. Again, I resolutely raised my hand. Dad had already made an impressive stovepipe hat for my previous cub scout costume. The authentic hat and my honest Abe looks made me a natural for the noble calling at hand. Thus, I became a mouthpiece of freedom as the great Abraham Lincoln.

Rehearsals were busy as many kids scrambled to learn their parts. Everyone felt important and a bit nervous too. Parents, teachers, students and a variety of guests filled the multi-purpose hall. The stage and microphones had somehow grown larger. The director patted my shoulder when it came time for Davy Crockett to blaze a new trail of progress across our panoramic stage of American events. My walk was steady and determination clear as I forged a way through untamed wilderness.

As I wore a distinguished beard and donned the hat of Lincoln, my young voice echoed through the auditorium, the words through time itself.

Four score and seven years ago…

Though originally spoken a century before, the full measure of Lincoln's Gettysburg Address was felt anew in the hearts of many. The conclusion of our American play brought resounding applause from proud parents, teachers and kids of all ages. Mother said we had all done well. The bold experience gave many a sense of something deep and moving. I quietly touched the stars of our classroom flag and began to imagine the brave hands that helped put them there.

Show and tell was always a fascinating time during grade school. You just never knew what some kids might bring for the marquee moment. I brought a beautiful bull snake. The fast little fellow and I first met in our desert jungle of wonders. He appeared to be searching for a friend, so I swooped in and presented myself. We looked into each other's eyes and something sweet happened. It was friendship at first sight.

Look mother, I found a pretty bull snake out back.

What are you going to do with it? she curiously asked.

Tomorrow is show and tell, so I'll take it to school.

How are you going to get it there?

Well, I'll make a nice home for it in a big jar.

Here's some sand and leaves so he'll be comfortable.

I'll make some holes in the jar lid with an ice pick for good air conditioning.

The lucky reptile then received a luxurious night stay in a five star snake hotel.

The next morning, I galloped to the garage to make sure my new partner was fully prepared for the unveiling presentation. I placed the jar in a brown paper bag for the bus ride to school. We didn't want to let the cat, or snake surprise, out of the bag too soon. When our fourth grade teacher invited kids to the front for show and tell, I politely let others go first. Anticipation bubbled within and the excitement was almost unbearable.

Donald, we're all curious, the teacher teased.

What did you bring?

The moment had arrived. I carefully removed my precious jar from the brown bag.

It's a snake! I swiftly declared.

Spontaneous squeals rolled through the classroom, unanimous among girls. The teacher seemed somewhat befuddled. She had a similar look when I previously announced that dad was going to paint her wagon. You see, mother and dad had recently attended a parent-teacher conference at school. Dad didn't fully agree with my teacher's progress assessment and future plan of action. I overheard him say to mother that if the teacher didn't change her ways, he was going to paint her wagon. Being a fine communicator, I relayed precisely the same message back to my teacher.

Oh, you shouldn't tell your teacher that, mother later informed me.

Why not, that's what he said, I reasoned.

Yes, but it's just not something you should tell your teacher, she explained.

Well, the cautious teacher kept a good distance from my trusted snake as she and the kids asked a few questions. Our level of excitement rose significantly during recess as I brought forth the jar to an active playground. A group of kids gathered as I demonstrated what my clever snake could do. Watch closely, I beckoned, this snake is trained to follow my finger. Our snake lay securely within the glass jar, fully focused on my finger. Each time I pointed at the little fellow and slowly raised my hand, he would obediently rise up. As I lowered my finger and instructed him to sit, again he would faithfully follow. A growing audience was impressed.

Can I try? an enthusiastic onlooker asked.

Well, he only does it for me, I explained.

Now the show needed to get bigger and better. In a moment of daring, I removed the lid. Like walking a tightrope without a safety net, I continued to move my finger along the jar. Then, I raised my hand too high and the sweet little snake lifted his head above the open rim. I quickly lowered my finger but the savvy snake had already sensed freedom and kept rising up. My nerves of steel suddenly melted and I dropped the showcase jar. My snake charming stature, along with the glass jar, shattered upon the playground pavement. A determined bull snake raced away as our popular partnership appeared over.

What to do?

I sprinted back to the schoolroom and searched for a new container in my quest to recapture the runaway reptile. All I could find was an empty bottle of Joy dishwashing liquid beneath the classroom sink. It would have to do. I quickly rinsed it and returned to a vast playground area. I searched in every direction, but he was gone.

Please God, help me find my snake.

After several long minutes, I spotted the lost creature in a nearby grass field. I decided to retrieve and carry him home where a safe release could be made. My weary little friend was carefully lifted and placed in the bottle of Joy. Once home, I gently jiggled a resilient reptile from the plastic bottle and watched him glide smoothly away. I glanced at the empty bottle of Joy and realized the little bull snake was probably now the cleanest snake around. The show was complete and I could tell we were both glad. A warm sunset drew our day of adventure to a close, but there was always next week … and a new show and tell.

My Melody Of Dreams

One of my earliest employment opportunities came from mother.

Donnie, there are gobs of armyworms in our lawn.

I'll pay you a penny for every worm you gather.

Mother's offer sounded pretty good. Every ten worms I found would be worth ten cents and you could buy a lot with a dime. If the worms cooperated, I could receive a juicy payday.

Yes mother, I'm your man.

Thus, I became a certified worm wrangler.

The primary tools of my trade were an empty olive jar along with paper and pen for tabulation. We had an abundant supply of writing pens around the house that were imprinted with the solemn words – Property of the U.S. Government. The grey pens had a small metal spring within that when taken apart could launch each pen capsule across the room like a rocket ship. I conducted several such test flights with great success. Though dad often worked at the Nevada Test Site, I wondered if we could somehow be in trouble for having so many official government pens in our possession. Fortunately, those men in black never did arrive to take away our small grey friends – uh, pens. With a keen eye and special pen at hand, I began an epic worm roundup.

Fortune smiled that sunny day and within an hour fifty worms wiggled in my jar. By afternoon, 215 had joined the happy harvest. Mother was amazed with my worm wrangling prowess and productivity. I then instituted a successful worm relocation program to a nearby area of open desert. By the following day, I had gathered and transported 500 squirming volunteers. I eagerly reported the milestone achievement to mother and was ready to receive a generous bounty.

500! she exclaimed.

Yes mother, my labors have been fruitful.

Here's five dollars and you worked hard to earn it, but from now on the pay rate will be a penny for every two worms, she explained.

That's only half a cent per worm, I pleaded.

Well, you're finding too many, so I can only afford to pay half as much going forward.

I quickly learned about supply and demand in action. When worm supplies were up, prices went down. I still gathered another 250 reluctant worms at a reduced retail rate before overall supply dwindled. A classic worm boom and bust had played out – and thus ended my brief career as a worm entrepreneur.

Some kids made lemonade stands while growing up, but I found a sweeter idea. Ice cream floats could really fill your tank on a sun soaked day. Now mother had enough supplies to satisfy a steady caravan of kids who came our way. Root beer floats with vanilla ice cream were a traditional favorite. We also drenched cold ice cream with orange or grape soda, which I called a purple cow. Twenty-five cents got every child, neighbor and friend a frosty smile. Everyone was warmly welcomed at our refreshing table of dreams. If someone didn't have a quarter, we gladly gave and shared the same. There was something about root beer floats that just seemed all-American. Those we made them for often became all-time friends.

As an enterprising lad, I discovered there really was gold in them thar hills, or rather aluminum in the form of castaway cans. A call of the Klondike swept through my mind as the news of cash for cans tickled my ears. Every aluminum can would fetch half a cent at the local recycling yards. Twenty cans could bring a dime and 200 a green dollar bill. The prospect of collecting cans jingled a pleasant tune as my mental and bicycle wheels continued to turn. I enthusiastically shared my industrious idea with mother and dad, who both served as co-chairman of the board. Each approved of the prosperous plan as dad also encouraged me to consider collecting copper. Electrical wire and copper plumbing parts were often discarded among scattered desert mounds. Some of the dump sites sat for years and I journeyed through them like a Spanish conquistador. During one expedition, I discovered a Peruvian silver bracelet with curious engravings. There was always something exciting to unearth.

My young eyes became seasoned at scanning a rich patchwork of desert dirt roads. One distant road was called Rainbow. I rode my dusty bike to the end of it and there found a copper pot of gold. The castaway copper gleamed brighter than gold as I carried it on home. Dad had a strong wood bench in our garage, covered with several working scars. He showed me how to safely remove the insulation surrounding my copper wire. I carefully cut and opened each outer shell. Like precious strands of lustrous pearl, brightly polished copper was soon revealed.

A variety of returnable soda bottles were also a special find. Orange Crush, Dr. Pepper, Pepsi, thick Coke and emerald green 7-up bottles, all were worth three to five cents each. Extra large bottles brought a dime. Many grocery stores paid cash for the sparkling desert gems. On the way home from shopping at Safeway, I sometimes asked mother to follow a road less travelled.

There's one over there! I hollered.

Mother would graciously stop as I bolted toward the prize. Sometimes, two or three green coke bottles would be resting together, waiting for someone to rescue them. I poured out the sand which had gathered through time and gave them new life.

Yes, we discovered great treasures in those days and perhaps some were more precious than gold.

Sand is plentiful in Southern Nevada. If it were gold, we'd all be wealthy. Mesquite bushes across an open landscape accumulated vast deposits of this desert gold or as we called it – blow sand. Each desert dust storm brought an incredible transfer of such wealth. Great quantities of blow sand were deposited in sandbanks around our property. Generous amounts were also distributed among a hidden network of pyracantha branches. Mother offered me a new job as blow sand removal specialist and I was hired at a rate of ten cents per wheelbarrow load. With a square point shovel, worn wheelbarrow and sweat soaked gloves, I became an eager prospector of desert gold. Each precious load of refined sand was carefully wheeled to an adjacent lot. Every flip of the barrow left a perfect mound of granular glory. The amount of golden sand transferred was enormous. It reminds me of Federal Reserve currency. We're not really sure where it comes from and very few realize where it actually goes.

Well, I cleared thirteen full loads of blow sand that day and gladly earned $1.30 in pay. I rested especially well that night as Mr. Sandman seemed to smile. He brought me a deep and peaceful dream as I slept for a very long while.

As a young feller, I found antique bottles to be a lot like people. Some are rather old and have colorful stories to tell. A rounded flask with pewter cap peered through my hands as it sat on my lap. It whispered a tale from ages ago when it traveled a trail few prospectors know. The bottle once held something other than milk as it kissed the old cowboy, he dreamt it was silk. With a grin on his face he drank the last drop, then cast it aside with a skip and a hop. In the hot desert sun it lay for a while, 80 years warmed with a wide Sonoran smile. Then dad picked it up with a kick and a grin, he raised it once more as it shimmered within. Now it sits on a shelf of memories past with others that share rich stories in glass. Of distant days not so long ago and those who once held and treasured them so.

An old chili pepper jar from a forgotten miner's camp was a violet jewel indeed. If colors could sing, as they sometimes do, purple was Pavarotti in spring. Dad noticed it there near a worn pickaxe where it slept for seasons and dreamed, of a day to be found and loved once again, to sparkle, glisten and gleam. He touched the old glass and brushed it all clean, with strong gentle hands he lifted and leaned. A rainbow of light enveloped that scene as a sweet purple vessel was found and redeemed. Did you also know that glass insulators once sang with a choir on tall wooden poles and telephone wires? They hummed a sweet tune through soft starlit nights and welcomed each morn as she offered her light. Each day adorned with emerald glass, they still sing in times both present and past.

A beautiful way to smile more often is through good music. Phyllis and Linda each learned to play the piano and we all shared a few sing-alongs together. Two of dad's favorite melodies were Aura

Lea and Danny Boy. Dad sometimes highlighted his musical gift by playing Moonlight Sonata on the piano and Ghost Riders on guitar. I especially enjoyed singing and sailed away with Around the World in 80 Days. My spirit was further lifted by the ever-inspiring music and words of Born Free. Almost every Christmas Season we joined our voices together in singing O Little Town of Bethlehem. Beautiful music just seems to inspire and lift everyone. Maybe we can add a few more verses in our daily melodies of life.

December always brought a warm spirit into our welcome home. The outdoor air was brisk, but a gentle glow surrounded the family hearth. Early in the season, mother and dad gathered us round. It was time to choose a Christmas tree. We set forth in a steady truck on our brief voyage of promise. The excitement of searching for a fragrant tree kept us warm in the cool evening breeze. Many of the trees offered a pleasing presence and we viewed all of them with gratitude. When a selection was made, we received our new tree with gladness and prepared for the journey home. The majestic tree soon stood prominently in a colorful stand of living water.

Frosted ornaments twirled in our hands as we reached for waiting branches to receive them. Joyous colored lights, which had slept since last Christmas, now glowed with renewed life. Each bright ornament seemed to shimmer amid the music of dancing light. Warm icicles embraced evergreen branches, glistening in time. Cheerful garland and twinkling tinsel also joined in a celebration of life. Dad then crowned our Christmas tree with an angel blue spire. Our eyes were touched with wonder and hearts with songs of hope.

Phyllis, Linda and I often sat before the brightly decorated tree immersed in imagination. Each would secretly choose an ornament of the moment and offer descriptive clues. We all tried to guess which delightful ornament the others had chosen. Colorful Christmas lights became even more beautiful with house lamps turned low. The growing anticipation of Christmas Eve sometimes required great stamina and emotional endurance. At times, I lay awake at night, wrapped in a restless blanket of frenzied possibility. I also thought of people in humble places who maybe didn't have so much and sincerely wished for them to have a special Christmas Day and every day.

We each had a decorative stocking set by the brick fireplace on Christmas Eve.

Had I been good enough during the past year?

I really wasn't sure. Maybe Santa didn't have a good memory and I would luck out.

My uncertainty was unsettling.

Please God, let Santa remember just the good things I did.

Christmas Eve did arrive and we all opened our wonderful presents. To my great surprise, mother and dad wheeled in a new bicycle as twinkling lights reflected from mirror-like handlebars. I eagerly sat upon the curved banana seat supported by a stylish sissy bar. Flared fenders, factory fresh wheels and untouched pedals caused my heart to race. This was a Corvette compared to the faded battlewagon I so often rode. I thanked mother and dad for the special surprise and they were happy, so much as I. December was warm in so many ways through wondrous nights and cherished days.

By the grand ol' age of ten, the high desert was still my home. Dirt roads stretched in every direction and were a natural fabric of life. Some led upward to elevated valley views, others through rocky washes amid endless skies of blue. Dust contrails rose across a dry horizon as distant travelers searched for their promised land. We too ventured where few had gone before. Now dad approached me with a bold new plan. Pop was very resourceful and his creative ideas were often well beyond the box. We could buy an old Volkswagen Beetle and transform it into a dirt lovin' Baja Bug. The versatile vehicle would be mine and I could pay for it over time. We could set goals and work on our creation together. Dad would teach me how to drive and a network of dirt, gravel and paved roads would be my schoolhouse.

Let's begin.

We soon found a 1960 Volkswagen looking for someone to love it. The grey bug had seen brighter days, but we both saw real potential and bought it for $150. I felt the lonely bug say thank you as we brought it on home. Mother liked it too, so we fully adopted the grateful grey beetle. I frequently visited and sat in it for a few days, so the bug would feel welcome and loved. Our bug had a hard time starting so we consulted a dune buggy doctor. It would need an engine transplant. We all agreed the delicate operation would lead to a much better quality of car life and proceeded forward with success.

We then performed some cosmetic surgery on the front and rear fenders. Dad drew lines along each curved surface and carefully removed excess material. The new cut-away fenders were sleek and sexy. We located a pair of steel studded snow tires for the back and matching oversize treads for the front. Dad showed me how to remove rusty lug nuts from well-worn wheels and clean the surface within. I applied several coats of stunning silver paint to a set of reborn rims. Polished chrome acorn nuts gave each wheel a glistening new smile. I tenderly installed super duty shocks and lubed every arthritic joint. We crafted a cut away engine with chrome exhaust and attached a bold iron skid plate. I proudly showed mother our bug's newfound muscle and she was thoroughly impressed.

Dad also instructed me on how to install a new AM radio from Sears. As I completed the task and turned some knobs, a clear signal was heard. I almost felt like Einstein humming a new melody of relativity. We chose a smooth chrome steering wheel with squishy foam grips as I sat several nights polishing it and my new driving skills. Now dad worked as a journeyman upholsterer in younger years and simply called the process "spitting tacks." The bug's sun cracked seat seemed to softly say – please don't forget about me. Pearl white leatherette on the back bench now looked like a million bucks. I chose leopard print terry cloth for the front and dad made a pair of snug seat covers that growled with explosive speed. Sky blue carpet covered the floorboard as we watched a dream come true. Many long days and oft late nights had brought our bug to bear.

The four speed figure H shifter was a piece of pie. Going in reverse was like pineapple upside down cake. The clutch, brake and gas pedals were like playing a sweet guitar, but with your feet. There was no doubt when the engine fired up and if anyone was asleep, well, they didn't need to be. I sat on a tall seat cushion to help me see over the steering wheel. Dad was my ever trusted co-pilot and air traffic controller in one. Mother went with us for an early ride but hollered way too much when I drove off-road. Hold on, I told her, but she hollered even more.

Go back to the road, she pleaded.

Dad realized that mother wasn't ready for all-terrain travel, so I returned to a level surface road.

That's better, she sighed in relief.

We baptized our bug in a glorious cloud of dust and confirmed it on a pleasant hillside climb. My good friend Sam also got to drive and gave us a thrilling rocky ride. He just needed a little more practice to smooth out those turns.

One summer day, dad and I drove toward the upper Spring Mountain Range. Be careful, mother said, as we prepared to leave. I gave her a hug and waved goodbye.

Please God, help us have a safe journey, I whispered.

On we drove, as a broad horizon stretched before us. Dad directed me as we traveled ever higher along unfamiliar roads. A rugged skyline of Juniper and Pinyon pine marked the way.

Suddenly, dad stretched forth his foot and stomped my brake pedal. We stopped almost instantly.

What happened? I wondered.

Back up slowly, he directed.

Just ahead of us was a quick and unseen turn on the gravel road. A steep rocky hillside lay below. Dad's view was more complete than mine and his quick response had saved the day.

We had many happy journeys together and our Baja Bug was like a best friend. Mother made some favorite photos of the Bug and I. She even made me a Baja Bug birthday cake with frosted doors and licorice wheels.

Yes, dad had some great ideas. Together we created and drove a dream.

But dreams are like that and all you have to do is begin…

"Home means Nevada, Home means the hills…" This is a chorus from the state song of Nevada which we often sang during our fifth grade school year. Those classroom renditions were actually pretty good. What really stirred our spirit were the forever inspiring melodies of America the Beautiful and My Country 'Tis of Thee. Each morning we stood and placed small hands over hopeful hearts as we offered our Pledge of Allegiance. Even at that young age, an espirit de corps seemed to prevail. This was also where I learned how to play the trombone. The first tune I could fully play was the classic Ode to Joy. Beethoven, however, was probably holding his ears. I soon performed for some relatives in California and they all applauded when I was done. Perhaps they were clapping more in relief than for my horn blowing skills. We've heard there are magnificent trumpets in heaven. I wonder if there are any trombones. If so, Gabriel will probably keep me away from them.

My fifth grade handwriting abilities fared somewhat better. Our fine teacher, Mr. Wilde, held quarterly penmanship contests for combined classes. All students would view several unnamed entries and then vote for the one they thought best. To my great surprise, Mr. Wilde made the stunning announcement that I had won. I proudly showed my parents the decorative certificate and kept it as evidence of my redemptive qualities. Our class then made a memorable field trip to Nellis Air Force Base to meet some visiting astronauts. Alan Shephard, the first American in space and also commander of the Apollo 14 mission to the moon, flew overhead in a streaking fighter jet. Upon landing, he and other guests greeted enthusiastic students near the plane. A few kids were prepared to request a personal signature. As Commander Shephard offered his hand, I also requested the famous astronaut's autograph. He gladly began with a beautiful letter A when my pencil lead broke.

Did I have another pencil or pen? he kindly asked.

I carried only one that day. It was special to meet a great man of space. Yet, I realized then how good it was to always have a backup pen and plan in place.

I was active as a Webelo Scout that year and looked forward to each new frontier. Mother and dad encouraged me as I received thirteen of the fifteen badges available. I still treasure that Webelos shoulder pin with tricolor ribbon awards. My friend Sam and I both blazed an exciting trail as Webelo Scouts during that growing time of life. Now Sam's family was very much Italian and his dear mother invited me to stay for lunch one day. She then set a warm plate of something called lasagna before me.

What was this new dish?

Please God, let this lasagna be something good and not make me sick.

I carefully raised a forkful and gently nibbled at the cheesy content. My taste buds quickly agreed this was not a foreign invader but a welcome guest indeed. Caution aside, I gobbled more as my tentative tasting became a frenzied feast.

Do you like the lasagna?

Yes ma'am, this is really good.

Would you like more?

Yes please, my euphoric tongue shouted.

I discovered a romantic love for lasagna and real Italian food that day. Thanks be to Sam and his wonderful mother for serving me that way. A tasty thought then stirred in my mind, I could become Italian–how delicious and divine!

Sam and I did a lot together as our birthdays and homes were ever near. Sometimes it just happens that way. We built bicycle ramps and made daring jumps that couldn't quite clear the Grand Canyon but sailed high over Southern Nevada sands. That go-kart sure was noisy as we raced a mile or two. Ping-pong kept us hoppin' for hours till we were through. We both had slingshot rockets and B-B guns to boot. We swam through endless summers and ran without our shoes. Board games, chess and fishing, bowling, horseshoes too–we did just about everything two young fellers could do. We sometimes sat and wondered what life might bring that day. The sunsets came so quickly, each season swept away. But friendships last forever, whatever life may bring. These moments are the treasures that make our hearts to sing.

Sports For All Seasons

A variety of sports can be good for everyone and bring smiles in every season. Dad was very athletic as a youth and punched his own sports ticket with Golden Gloves boxing. It was only natural when he gave me two new pair of semi gold gloves. We both pulled on our padded pounders and stared each other down. A bout for the ages was about to begin. Mother snapped photos like a hungry sportswriter as Phyllis rang an imaginary bell. Dad proudly knelt on both knees to equalize his great height advantage. He smiled with confidence, wiggled his gloves and waved me closer. I was too smart for that and danced around our living room ring. My precious head was just too valuable, so I kept the champ at bay. Those savvy skills earned me a well-deserved draw from the ringside judge. Mother may have favored me slightly as I raised my gloves in triumph.

I then focused on somewhat easier prey – Phyllis and Linda. They didn't possess my fancy footwork or stunning speed. I could easily whoop their puddin and raise my record too.

Would you like to box with me? I innocently inquired.

Step into the ring of my web, the shy spider softly said.

Please God, let them say yes.

No thank you was their reply.

I promise we'll just hit gloves and not your pretty eyes.

Still, no takers. Ultimately, most of my bouts were with a flexible boxing stand. Thus, my sterling record and boxing career, much like those of Rocky Marciano, remained perfect and undefeated.

Mother and dad also decided to toss me a new football for Christmas. I cradled the little wonder as a precious child, then bolted for outdoor fields of glory. The San Francisco 49ers uniform and helmet from Sears made my new calling official. Now dad understood the value of a good helmet. His parents had given him new headgear when he played football at Burbank High. Dad sometimes played the position of quarterback and also excelled as a kicker. During practice, he noticed a teammate who didn't have a protective helmet and graciously offered his own as vigorous action continued. Well, one particular play dad and another fellow were running towards each other like two oncoming trains. Dad somehow forgot he wasn't wearing that new headgear as the other guy grinned, exposing two enormous front teeth. An abrupt collision echoed around the outdoor field as both athletes lay dazed from a thunderous impact. Dad realized he now had some extra front teeth–two of them in his forehead. The other guy was missing a couple.

Dad was rushed home where his folks looked on in disbelief. The whopper sized teeth were deeply embedded in his noggin. A doctor was called and quickly arrived. Dad's sister, Norma Jean, held a steady light as the doctor grabbed ahold of each tooth with strong pliers. The doc had a whale of a time pulling those thumper teeth out and the whole operation seemed greatly in doubt. After several tough tries, each embedded tooth finally gave up the ghost. Blood gushed forth like Old Faithful from dad's forehead and Norma Jean passed out.

Eventually, they were able to slow the bleeding and dad lay recovering with a hurricane size headache.

Dad showed me the scars on his aging forehead as I put on my new helmet.

Does it still hurt? I quietly asked.

Not any more, time and a little luck were good medicine, he recalled.

Did the other guy get his teeth back? I wondered.

I don't think so, dad said with a resilient smile.

Sometime later, I was playing flag football at school. I sprinted thirty yards toward the end zone, turned and yelled, "throw me the ball–I'm open!" There was an abrupt collision. Every bell on the North American continent suddenly rang and echoed through my mind. I had run head first into a large iron goalpost. My bare head and trailing body were like an inbound comet hurtling towards earth. I lay in the end zone wondering which planet I had landed upon. Eventually, I returned to a realm of reason and could once again count to four. I discovered through personal experience the great value of a good helmet and also of keeping your eye on immovable goals.

Spring was a pleasant season and mother always planted brilliant flowers. I helped dad plant a dome-shaped backboard and bright orange hoop above our garage door. Basketball was a great sport that everyone could enjoy. Wanda's mother, Alma, was a terrific ball player on her Texas high school team. She also competed in county track and field events, winning several awards. Alma was good enough to have attended college with a sports scholarship, but chose to marry her sweetheart, E.L. Wilson Jr. and start a family. Together they raised

Margie, Wanda and Wilma, three of the best lifetime blue ribbons a couple could receive.

Well, dad attached a silky white net to our basketball rim and showed me how to make some sweet swishes. We also practiced a fine technique of shooting foul shots. I could almost sense Jerry West in every arching release and quick jump shot. Yet, I somehow became more proficient at committing fouls than actually scoring from the charity stripe. Phyllis and Linda joined me for a few games of HORSE where I developed an unbeatable hook shot. If a half court throw missed the backboard, it usually struck the garage door with a loud boom. Since the atomic test site wasn't too far away, we were already familiar with those kind of sounds and really didn't mind.

Now dad had played basketball and achieved distinction in several sports while yet in junior high. He was somewhat of a young Jim Thorpe in all around events. Yet, his back was often sore from a serious helicopter crash at the Test Site when I was about two. An eventual spinal fusion left him decidedly less flexible than Gumby. Still, he could drain the bucket at will and block some of my best shots. Complete body strength was a plus in basketball and dad knew just how to elevate our game.

Weightlifting is an ancient sport and dad didn't attend those first Olympic Games in Greece. He did however grow up in Southern California and developed a chiseled physique lifting weights in the area now known as Muscle Beach.

We wrote the book on weightlifting, he sometimes mused.

Dad created successful workout routines during his brief days at UCLA. He also lifted some iron while attending SMU at Dallas. There in the school gym, he met fellow student Doak Walker, college football's Heisman Trophy winner of 1948. Doak gave dad his personal pair of sweatpants which he then wore in those humble days of glory.

Now I had seen a few of those Charles Atlas bodybuilder ads inviting me to become like Hercules. Was it possible? Dad was really good at building things. Perhaps he held a golden key for unlocking my powerful physical potential. Dad soon recruited all of us, including mother, to join his Nevada version of Muscle Beach in the desert. Once again, Sears was the go-to place for current sports equipment. We brought home a complete weight training set of brilliant barbells and smart dumbbells. Dad introduced each of us to the major muscle groups and his three day a week workout schedule.

To build a muscle up, you've got to break it down, he explained.

Ten reps a set and three sets per group was a solid formula for steady success. Mother chose improved muscle tone as her ultimate goal. Phyllis sought pectoral gains through devoted lifts and figurative change. I envisioned boulder size biceps and Tarzan like triceps. After five days, I flexed my weary arms in front of a complimentary mirror. Were there any meteoric changes yet? I just couldn't tell.

Please God, help my muscles become big and strong, I secretly sighed.

Mother, are my biceps any bigger than before?

Maybe a little, she surmised.

Well, I'll just need to keep lifting more weights, I replied.

I often lay on that incline bench pressing weighted bars amid cricket chirps toward distant stars. Building muscle and strength is a steady climb, as desire and effort yield progress in time.

Swimming was a sparkling sport in our warm world of summer. Mother encouraged me early to jump over streams of doubt and into a deep blue sea. Together we ventured forth to the wonderful YMCA and a bright pool of promise. Mother smiled as I dog paddled my way from Wiggler to the advanced stage of Tadpole. New waves of opportunity began to crest around me. Could it be, a future life as aquanaut amidst a living sea? Now having a pool at our new desert home was truly a welcome wonder. We had previously played with a garden hose or Slip N Slide in those slower days of summer. This was like having part of the Pacific Ocean in your own backyard. Jumping into a freshwater lagoon encircled by concrete reefs just had to be fun.

Dad displayed acrobatic somersault flips and delivered thunderous cannonballs from the springboard. Mother completed several dives of distinction and Phyllis perfected the back dive. I performed elegant and lofty swan dives. We all cheered as Linda leapt with a variety of Heinz 57 style jumps and successfully landed within the pool. We splashed our way through summer days with buckets of fun-filled games. There was water raft racing, surfboard balancing and Olympic speed swimming. Our California cousin, Dean, was an exceptional endurance swimmer. Water polo, underwater gymnastics, hand walking and of course, bouncing the giant beach ball, topped our bowl of aquatic fun. We played upon the high seas with deep pools of energy, swam in an endless summer sun and watched the days drift on.

We also served up a warm dish of summer fun with sweet slices of volleyball on the run. Our beachfront net stood far from Malibu coves as sun bleached sand swirled and swept around our toes. Almost every jump and skyward volley sent the scuffed leather ball on a different journey. Our patchwork net endured as a movable continental divide. A great way to score was through serving, some quick adjustments and a determination to follow through. Can you dig it? Mother often poured generous cups of Kool-Aid to help tame the bold summer days. Volleyball in the arid Nevada sun gave each of us a perfect Bakelite patina that lasted well beyond the coming autumn breeze. Soon, the leaves of summer turned to fall, green to gold, the seasons all.

Every young lad can dream of swingin some lumber and hitting home runs. Mother and dad bestowed a sweet Louisville Slugger upon my open hands with a direct commission from above … Take a swing son, but let me step back before you do.

A large softball and stiff leather glove accompanied my brave new bat. Dad then tossed what appeared to be an incoming ostrich egg toward my statuary position. I promptly tried to defend myself with a mighty swing. Great momentum carried me almost full circle as the global wonder passed by.

Be patient and let the ball come to you, dad explained.

With eager anticipation I waited for the next pitch. Again, my sizzling bat was just too fast for the slower softball.

Try again, dad confidently said.

This time a majestic swing almost met the ball.

How many tries do I get?

Usually about three, but we'll keep going.

This really was a smart softball that evidently knew how to avoid getting hit. Finally, the bat, boy and ball all got together at the same time as I struck a solid grounder. My tilted shoulders quickly squared with every crack of the hungry bat.

That's how you do it, dad nodded, just takes practice.

It seemed I was already a natural at fielding and throwing that spherical gem.

We all soon gathered on some desert turf of sage and sand. First base was a native creosote bush, second a weathered quartz stone, third a square piece of plywood and home a plastic green plate. A small pitcher's mound was formed of high-grade Nevada dirt. Our desert diamond wasn't set in Fenway Park, but seemed just as glorious. Linda even wore her favorite pair of bright red socks for the first game. Dad tossed a ceremonial pitch as Phyllis took in centerfield. Mother called strike and Linda soon appealed. Yes, softball can be a strikingly fun sport. We all get to stand and take our swings, whatever the season of life may bring.

You're up, You're out, You're safe, You're home ... whatever the call, you're never alone.

The desert can hold untold secrets and timeless treasures for a young feller. I sometimes found things from lost civilizations and made incredible scientific discoveries. There was always something to bring home and show mother.

Look at what I found!

An excited hand presented her with a well-worn and slightly rusted piece of steel. Mother carefully examined the U-shaped artifact and offered an informative appraisal.

Looks like a horseshoe, she declared.

Did somebody loose it, I wondered.

Someone's horse may have, she explained.

Is the horse ok? I intently asked.

Probably, sometimes they just loose a shoe, mother assured me.

I then looked at both of my small feet. Sure would notice if I lost one of my shoes!

The horse probably got a new one, she calmly replied.

Besides, some people think that horseshoes bring good luck.

I was glad to hear that and within a week had found another.

Several seasons later, dad introduced us to the ring dingin sport of horseshoes. I observed four large shoes that appeared to have come from a mighty big horse. They were specially made for pitching at iron stake targets set firmly in the ground. If a horseshoe landed and remained close enough to the slake, you scored a point. If the lucky shoe leaned against the iron goal, you scored two. The real prize was to encircle the target with your designated shoe. That was a ringer worth three points and not as easy to do. The more we played, the better each of us became. We pitched, threw, leaned and laughed, then slept and tossed some more. There were hundreds of ringers along the way and plenty of points to score. Maybe there are horseshoes in heaven. They say Jesus will return riding a faithful horse and we'll be able to hear Him come. I hope there are enough ringers in life before our time is done.

Tetherball could be designated an Olympic sport. Almost every playground offers a dynamic universe of these orbiting satellites on a string. Some enterprising company could connect them to eco-friendly windmills, thus generating an enormous amount of clean energy. Dad decided to dig an exploratory hole in our yard for such a tetherball pole. He then gave me a shovel and some excellent instructions on how to proceed. Upon completion of my manual backhoe efforts, we planted a tall galvanized pole and fertilized it with fresh cement.

93

We'll let the pole set for a few days before attaching the long cord and new ball, dad explained.

The superintendent was then informed that I already knew about that.

Each day, I secretly touched our tetherball tree to see how strong it was getting.

You didn't go out there and already press against the pole? dad sneakily inquired.

I shook my head a little sideways then up and down at the same time, kind of like an elusive tetherball in flight.

It's important to let the concrete cure, he reminded me.

Well, I already knew that.

The sun soon rose on a new day and it was time to attach the sleek winding rope and pristine ball. No further instructions were needed. I quickly sent the swaying ball sailing in almost endless circles. I then realized that one of the toughest things in life was to have been born a tetherball. Occasionally, it fought back by rounding the pole too fast and smacking me in the face. I spent several July days greeting the ball this way. Over time, we became trusted friends and treated each other with greater respect. If I skipped playing a day or two, I could tell the sun crusted ball had truly missed me. We talked of many things during our time together.

After several months of vigorous activity in a relentless Mojave sun, something happened. I addressed my special friend with a solid serve and he instantly broke free from the dangling cord. I stood in shock, then carefully retrieved my broken ball.

I'm sorry, I whispered, while looking upon the ball with grief.

I quickly ran for first aid and found a full roll of scotch tape. I courageously tried reattaching the broken eyelet to a frayed rope. Alas, my trusted tetherball had gone the way of all the world. It was bound to happen someday, I reasoned.

Perhaps, we should all observe a national be kind to tetherballs week. My best advice for potential tetherball athletes is still this – Always try and hit the ball and not the iron pole … having experienced both of these, I prefer the softer goal.

Some believe the crackin game of croquet rolled forth from France, but the Brits beg to differ. Others say those lucky Irish were in on it before the British took their first swing. Even the Scots enjoyed whacking those wooden balls around the countryside. Everyone, especially the English, seems to agree, it's a jolly good game. Dad thought so when he brought home a colorful rack of croquet balls and mallets to match. We gathered round the backyard lawn as dad, our acting Earl of Edinburgh, proclaimed the official rules. Each of us received a large striped ball and sturdy mallet. The goal was to successfully strike your ball through a series of narrow wickets and on to ultimate victory. This appeared much easier than trying to hit an egg size golf ball with one of those smaller spindly clubs. The best part was trying to hit someone else's ball with your own, then receiving a free whack to send theirs careening off course.

Please God, let me hit Linda's ball, so I can send it to Mars.

My humble prayer was answered and Linda wailed as I sent her hapless ball sailing toward a cinder block wall. I henceforth drilled dad's lucky ball well beyond the soft green sod. I just couldn't pounce on mother's cheerful ball and often let it roll on by. As I took delight playing demolition derby with most everyone else's ball, Phyllis made steady progress passing through each of her arched goals. I soon realized that it wasn't how many times you knocked someone else off course, but how many goals you actually achieved that won the day.

Yes, ol chap, croquet is a smashing sport, one that helped me become a better sport ... and isn't that a great part of every sport.

There is an ancient sport where feathered arrows fly and mighty bows still bend beneath an azure sky. Archery, as Cupid can attest, is an engaging sport for all ages. I received my first bow and arrow set around the independent age of five. Mother instructed me to have plenty of fun, but not shoot the house up too much in the glorious process. I quickly armed myself with a colorful bow and full quiver of suction cup arrows. The smooth tv screen made a good target and my bow skills were soon sharpened. It was now time to hunt the mysterious indoor forests where wild game was often seen. Phyllis and Linda frequently fed on the open dining room range or sometimes in the high country of a nearby kitchen. I patiently waited behind an outcropping of table rocks where grazing prey could easily be viewed.

Please God, help me hit the target before it gets away.

With a clear eye and steady hand, I drew the faithful bow. The flight of my rubber tipped arrow was true and Linda squealed as it swiftly followed through. Hurry, a second shot may fell the wounded critter before it flees away. My expert marksmanship was simply amazing.

Donnie shot me with another arrow, she instantly howled.

Please stop shooting arrows at your sister, mother implored.

We all reached a treaty and I agreed to lay down my bow in peace.

Grandma Ann and Grandpa Earnie then returned from an extensive trip up north. They brought back generous offerings of turquoise and rose-colored beads for Phyllis and Linda. To me, the Great Chief, they brought a beautifully feathered headdress and brightly painted drum. With great pleasure, they placed the ornate symbol of respect and wisdom upon my humble head. The sky blue and pure white feathers spread forth above my brow as a noble hawk in flight. I promptly sat upon the Great Plains of our backyard grass and began pounding the sacred calfskin drum. Rivers of Native American heritage flowed through my devoted hands as our little drum echoed across the Dakotas and into Canada beyond. From that moment, I no longer counted sheep at night, but endless herds of buffalo.

Years later, my good friend Sam handed me his strong new archery bow. I was more than ready to demonstrate my natural skills. His dad had wisely placed the targets a good distance from their home. I drew the splendid bow as Ulysses and quickly released a dynamically crafted arrow. The remote target appeared frozen in time.

Did I score a direct bullseye?

Better clean your glasses, Sam smiled.

You didn't even hit the target or backstop bale of hay.

What? Maybe I didn't figure for Kentucky windage.

Donzo, there's not even an autumn breeze this afternoon, he laughed.

Maybe my renown archery skills needed some fresh polish.

Indeed, man, bow and arrow could become and flow as one.

But until that time ... Sam bravely stood about fifteen feet behind.

Sam and I often shook hands as we reached across his army green ping pong table. The battle-scarred surface bore witness to marathon matches that could go on for hours. Many of the shots we made were beyond fantastic. I believe some could never be created again, not even by God Himself. We knew nothing of arthritis or quickly passing years. Our hearts were full of gusto and time was never near. Once I turned an ankle and felt an ache or two. The hurt was gone in moments, it passed as most pains do. We played for endless hours till sunlight slipped away as bonds of ping pong brothers endured the passing days.

Now tennis is a lot like ping pong, you just have to play with bigger paddles. Those serving usually address their opponents with great kindness and respect. I often heard them say 15-love and 30-love. There was so much love expressed by those playing tennis, you couldn't help but feel good. I think that's what Jimmy Connors and John McEnroe were really trying to say during their special tennis events. Many of the balls we volleyed were bright yellow or vivid orange. Depending on which ball was served, we always seemed to be reaching for a California lemon or running after a Florida orange. All in all, tennis is a tender sport. The more you love your opponent, the more points you can score.

Now Old Man Winter can be seen making the rounds just about everywhere, even in a place like Las Vegas. It was during one such frigid season that dad took the fever, a frenzied bowling fever to be sure. Dad discovered Grandpa Earnie's high-top bowling shoes perched within a dusty closet. They appeared to be from a bygone era, yet whispered with an ageless soul. Off we sped to a quaint shoe repair shop at the local Wonder World. There we clanged a countertop bell, hoping that someone was home. A salty maestro suddenly emerged from the drawn curtain surrounded by a vast audience of attentive shoes. Dad offered him the old leather tops with dark frayed laces.

Can you bring them back to life? he asked with a tender smile.

The elderly shoe sage gently caressed the deep worn leather with a strong hand as he briskly stroked a blue-grey beard with the other.

Haven't seen a pair of these for ages, he declared in admiration.

Yes, I'll give these some special care, strong new soles and softer leather.

Several days later, amid great anticipation, dad and I returned to that shoe shop of dreams. Our new friend brought forth a magnificent pair of reborn bowling shoes. Every other pair of waiting footwear seemed to kneel in humble respect. Dad was thrilled and his fever began to clear.

Let's go bowling, he readily announced, as Wonder World shoppers drew near.

I soon realized you could score more points bowling than in a game of football, baseball, hockey or just about any other sport. Everyone could rack up points with extra fun to spare. There were, however, a few exceptions. Linda went bowling with the girl scouts and scored just eleven points. I'm ever grateful that she and I didn't receive the same bowling DNA. Every week, we piled in the blue Mercury and headed for some local bowling lanes. Upon arrival, we scrambled with youthful vigor for an alley entrance. Open doors heralded thunderous events from within, drawing us ever closer to an epicenter of activity. Perfect lanes of polished opportunity reached out to greet us. Racks of rolling atomic balls jostled nearby. Some were speckled, others had stars, a few brightly colored and all bore scars. I eagerly bounded beside long rows of potential winners, viewing each as a ready racehorse.

Dad had a deliberate approach to releasing the ball and tried to put as he described, some English on it. I'm not sure what language my ball spoke but seemed to often hear it say–please release me, let me go. I preferred a power throw straight to the pins and clapped with approval as they scattered and fell. The automatic pin racks did get an occasional pounding and I asked dad how people bowled in those earlier days before modern technology.

Well, the bowling lanes were similar, but someone had to work behind the scenes as a pinsetter.

Dad then revealed that he, as a young boy, had worked part-time setting pins.

Did you ever get hit in the head by any bowling pins or bouncing balls?

Oh yeah, he quickly replied. You just had to take cover before the ball arrived.

Did people ever give you a tip?

Yes, they would sometimes toss a dime down the alley if you did a good job setting their pins.

I think dad had a unique enjoyment of and appreciation for the sport of bowling, especially since he didn't have to gather and set pins anymore. Every time he walked upon that perfect narrow lane with Grandpa Earnie's favorite shoes–the ones that bore his name ... some bowling angels cheered above and many young hearts too, he made a special score in life, the best a dad could do.

Breaking Through

Dad often showed me the value of hard work through example and opportunity. I was almost eleven when a large covered reservoir was to be built near our home. Dad decided to visit the on-site superintendent in my behalf. Was there perhaps a part-time job his hard-working son could do on weekends to gain valuable experience and earn a little money? There was indeed an important job that needed to be done. An enormous crater had already been dug and extensive gridworks of rebar were placed across the lower inclines. A steady train of cement trucks rolled like loyal worker bees to and from the active site. Massive cement sidewalls would soon be formed and placed upright in narrow channels called keyways. The superintendent needed someone who could fill the vital keyways with water to help strengthen and cure the concrete. I guess cement is somewhat like cheese and becomes stronger with age.

Every keyway channel within the vast reservoir would need to be watered twice a day on weekends. The hoses pulled along each side of the reservoir appeared long enough to serve an aircraft carrier. The work wasn't easy and pay was ten dollars per weekend. Could they depend on me to get the job done? Well, I got those reservoir channels flowing like a Louisiana Bayou and kept em all watered. Now freshly poured cement has a lingering sweet smell. If anyone ever asked what cologne I wore back then, I could easily have said it was Cement #6.

A few months later, the great project was complete. I was grateful for that part-time job dad helped me receive. It added to a growing reservoir of lifetime experience.

Moving on from grade school to junior high was like being called up to the mid-majors. Cashman Junior High with its circular design and curving hallways reminded me of the Starship Enterprise. I was suddenly transported into a bustling galaxy of charming girls and platform shoes. The large cafeteria was light-years beyond the simple hot dog and milk menu of grade school. There were several exotic entrees which featured burritos, tacos, pizza, meatloaf and potatoes or chicken with fries, just to name a classic few. The school burritos were actually pretty good and could have rivaled any military MRE. The all-purpose hot sauce packets did contain several unknown ingredients which I don't believe science ever fully identified. They may forever remain one of life's greatest mysteries. Those thick chocolate shakes were simply outstanding and should be considered a staple of every student's well-being. I discovered a direct correlation between the consumption of chocolate shakes and a significant increase in student performance. These findings were independently verified through extensive personal research.

As I often excelled during lunch, my teeth left a unique impression on every delicious item. If ever an apple were left behind, the part I chomped was obviously mine. Over time, some of my front teeth had shifted like the San Andreas Fault. I didn't mind my dental appearance, but mother offered to have me visit a smiling orthodontist. Now I was pretty good at opening my mouth and gave the good doctor a long ahh. He poked around my cavernous gumline and saw great potential. His sweet assistant then created some cherry flavored plaster casts of my wayward teeth. Congratulations Don, you're a challenging yet prime candidate for full orthodontic braces. Mother and I agreed with Dr. Zeiger as he crafted a durable plan of progress.

Every few weeks, I returned to see Dr. Z and those cute technicians. They lowered me back in large dental chairs as I gazed at the ceiling above. Lovely scenic posters had been placed above each relaxing chair. One portrayed a simple country road leading toward a peaceful sunlit home. Another featured a small girl feeding some fuzzy yellow ducklings. Yet another displayed a vibrant rainbow breaking through a temporary storm. Each visit with Dr. Zeiger was inspiring as his bright pliers and beautiful posters left moving impressions.

Unexpected opportunities sometimes present themselves and so it was during my first year of junior high school. Political fervor swept the halls as our Nevada Constitution instructor announced an election for seventh grade class president and key supporting offices.

Should I run for President?

Phyllis and Linda had already blazed a successful trail through junior high and were then elected to serve on student councils in high school.

You just might win, they urged.

Run Donnie, Run!

We'll even help you create some neat campaign signs.

Their voices of support spurred me on. Mother offered to help with campaign supplies and dad wondered if I might someday become a Senator. My girlfriend stood by me as I consulted with other friends and a potential campaign manager.

Alright, I'm in!

Our home became a busy hive of election activity. We made posters of every size with a variety of appealing messages. Phyllis sketched a portrait of my freckled face and placed aluminum foil as braces over the teeth. Her original slogan read, "Don't be scared – Vote for Don Brady." I bravely stood atop a classroom table in the circular hall and plastered it on the ceiling. Linda created a large poster with a unifying message, "Let's bring students Together – Vote Brady." I handed out stacks of valuable campaign ads to passing students and felt a surge of rising momentum. I tried to keep campaign promises to a minimum but did recommend that chocolate shake prices at the cafeteria be lowered for everyone.

Election day finally arrived and mother got me to school a couple hours early. I quickly covered central halls and classroom doorways with a final titanic wave of election material. Now Doug was also running for class president and his pre-election popularity was near 100%. We gave our final speeches and Doug received overwhelming applause. My confidence began to waver as I sensed a possible rout coming on. As votes were tallied, the result became clear. Doug had won in a seismic landslide. Even Steve, my campaign manager, voted for the other guy.

I didn't think you'd win, he explained.

Well, we ran a good campaign and came up a little short … Ok, I got trounced. Maybe, I could run for President again. Surely, there would be even greater opportunities on the bright road ahead. Perhaps a flowing banner with inspiring words could lead us in triumph.

For Freedom and Liberty every day, it's Donald J. all the way!

Just inside the entrance to our school, stood an inspiring display of historical documents called the Freedom Shrine. Some of the greatest proclamations to ever come forth from the furnace of America's freedom greeted students, teachers and visitors each new day. There on polished display were exact replicas of The Declaration of Independence, The Bill of Rights, The Gettysburg Address and several other bedrock documents of our beloved nation. Gazing upon the honored signatures of such noble men and remembering the courageous women who stood beside them was truly inspiring.

A nice man who worked there smiled and asked my name.

Don Brady, I quietly replied.

He didn't seem to clearly hear my first name.

Well, Tom Brady, you have a wonderful day.

Whether Don or Tom Brady, he was close enough.

Standing near the Freedom Shrine, we all felt like patriots.

As I passed by the school reception area, an enthusiastic photographer waved me near. He and a few officials were snapping some pictures for a new yearbook. Would I be willing to stand with the Dean of Students for a few photos? There was to be a very special shot of the Dean in action. I would lean forward as Mr. Addington held a large wooden paddle behind me. A famous photo of me receiving that swat from the smiling Dean soon appeared in our school yearbook. It became an overnight sensation.

Hey, aren't you that guy getting the swat?

Could you sign my yearbook?

I began carrying extra pens to fulfill all the requests. You see, life offers each of us special moments and distinct roles to play. Some of the best may greet us in rather unusual ways.

At the prime age of twelve, an unusual whirlwind of energy lifted my rising shoulders. About that time, mother noticed a small sidewalk sign pointing towards a new path of confidence. I wasn't old enough to join the Air Force but could become a moving force through the swift art of karate. Everyone would respect me if my hands, feet, elbows and maybe even my head became registered as dangerous weapons. Sign me up. Each student received a crisp karate uniform or gi. I stood at full attention in my new gi, brimming with enthusiasm and excitement. Our teacher, whom we respectfully addressed as Sifu, was a nice yet firm man. He introduced each new student to the class and told them the rules. Like West Point and other places of purposeful instruction, there was a chain of command and path to follow. Our journeys of discovery also held potential for great learning and reward.

The first day we learned to always remove our shoes and socks when entering the dojo. The large karate hall was ever blessed with a fragrant smell of feet – a lot of them. As a class, we bowed to Sifu and he to us, kindly acknowledging one another. That simple act of showing respect seemed to ennoble others and oneself. We learned to always face an opponent and never look away. Even when bowing, focus on the eyes. Sifu presented me with a perfectly folded crisp white belt. I firmly wrapped and cinched it around a newfound body of forged steel.

We practiced front kicks, side kicks or yoko geri, back kicks, roundhouse, alternate and double kicks, just about enough kicks to span Route 66. Our class released a flurry of kicks and chorus of karate yells that often shook the building. A large karate bag swung anchored from the ceiling and I greeted it frequently during each workout. The bag became a favorite of mine, especially since it didn't kick back. There were also many hand and arm techniques to grasp. The combination of these strikes and movements flowed with dramatic precision. Sifu taught us a progression of powerful moves which he called the Butterfly Ram. We learned and practiced each sequence until knowing them in full. Those martial art movements made a lasting impression on my twelve year old mind and body. I can quickly perform several key elements from memory even today. So, when I'm 93 don't mess with me. I'll still be able to dazzle you with the Butterfly Ram.

One bold day, Sifu had a special announcement for everyone. There would be an in school karate tournament for all students and ranks of his combined classes. Now Sifu competed in several tournaments himself, having won matches with some of the top-ranked athletes in the world. He sometimes served as a bodyguard for Howard Hughes, Muhammad Ali and others, but kept a low profile about that. We had truly drawn from a deep well of learning and experience. I was unsure of my overall abilities but jumped in the tournament anyway. Parents were also encouraged to attend and cheer their brave kids on.

Each participant who landed a significant strike to their opponent would receive a point. Sifu held a small flag and motioned toward each student as they scored. The first to accumulate three points was declared winner of that match. I was paired with another white belt and we were deemed about equal in ability. We bowed to each other and a signal was given to begin. Each of us scored, but somehow I reached three points first and was awarded the match. In the second round, I was to face a girl they called the Tank. She was a yellow belt and her stare alone almost knocked me over. They say you are what you eat and I must have had chicken that day. I offered a sincere silent prayer.

Please God, let this be over quickly and don't let me get hurt.

Sifu gave a signal and the Tank charged forward to meet me. If only we could kiss and call it a draw, but I guess that wasn't to be. To my relief, she scored quickly. I then spun around several times, launching wild back kicks. To everyone's surprise, including the judge, I scored. Maybe there was a chance, but I still felt way over my head. Mercifully, she landed two more scoring shots and it was over, but I was still alive!

Sifu also showed us an effective technique for breaking boards. When you unleash a kick, follow through with the ball of your foot. Don't point your toes at the board, that could be unfortunate. Several students tried and some were successful. It often took multiple kicks to ultimately break through.

Don, are you ready to break your first board?

Yes, Sifu.

I boldly stepped forward with a tinge of uncertainty.

My first try didn't succeed. Neither did the second and my foot was feeling it.

Are you ready to try again? he asked.

I'll wait for another day, was my reluctant reply.

A new day did arrive and I felt ready as the class looked on.

See yourself breaking through the board, Sifu counseled.

He gripped the wood firmly as I attacked it. The board won.

Try again, he encouraged.

I did and the board broke. A rainbow of small bruises appeared on the side of my ankle, yet I felt like having just received A Medal of Honor.

Sifu, would you sign my first broken board?

He signed with a smile of wisdom and I kept the two halves of that board. They remind me of how we can do hard things even when the outcome doesn't seem certain.

Keep trying my friend, for every day is a new day in the grand dojo of life.

Challenging opportunities are like glowing embers in a quiet fire. They have the power to ignite silent dreams and carry us well beyond desired goals. A new coach at school announced the creation of a cross country track team. His words sparked a desire within to run where few might go. I soon bought some red satin running shorts and royal blue track shoes. I may not have been that fast, but sure looked like I was going somewhere. We began running at a nearby high school. The quarter mile oval track and outdoor bleachers seemed to anticipate our arrival. The ready course fueled my desire and was made to be run. The first practice I ran eight laps or two brisk miles. I then began to set goals and increase the distance. Two miles became three and were soon eclipsed by four.

Increase gradually and build up steadily, coach relayed as I throttled on by.

I now wanted to run twenty laps, a full five miles without stopping.

Could I do it? Silently, I asked God to help me endure and not keel over while trying. The first time I broke through the five mile threshold, an unexpected feeling of euphoria flowed through my body. My legs felt like they could keep on running forever and it almost seemed unnatural to slow down. My body and mind were driven ever onward … like a blazing chariot of fire.

My energetic entrée of distance running was complimented with a variety of vigorous side dishes on the junior high menu. Physical Education offered a flavorful spectrum of activity highlighted by an all-around fitness challenge. Everyone did push-ups, pull-ups, sit-ups and a couple kids even did throw-ups, we all participated. Now Mike was a rather fit fellow and he decided to do as many continuous sit-ups as could be mustered. After quite some effort, he completed an astounding 1000 verified crunches. His phenomenal feat set a new sit-up record for our junior high.

How do you feel? I asked.

Happy but really sore, he reflected.

I also discovered sit-ups to be a natural strength and decided to go for the gold.

After preparing myself for the eventful day, I approached an open field.

Coach, I'm ready to start.

A volunteer held the hand counter as I began my sit-up marathon. I completed 500, then surpassed the 600 plateau and could have done many more. I thought about Mike and really didn't want to break his record. Besides, my volunteer counter looked almost as tired as I was. So, I gladly settled for second place on a distinguished roll of sit-up champions and you know, sometimes second place is a great place to be.

After school bowling leagues were ever popular during junior high and kids all around Las Vegas flocked to join them. Those were the days of acrylic clackers on a string, but flinging a Brunswick bowling ball was really my favorite thing. Sam and I promptly enlisted as volunteers in the Bantam Minors League. We boldly charged ahead as Rough Riders through the plains and answered every bugle call that rolled from West Hill Lanes. We called our motley band of five the Alley Cats. Every week we rolled against another team and there were many. One fine day, I bowled a 186 and received an American Junior Bowling Congress game patch. The high game and a rare split I picked up were listed in the sports section of our local newspaper. My name and lucky accomplishments were noted in fine print, yet it felt like having them boldly appear on Mt. Rushmore.

Our hungry Alley Cat crew was pleasantly surprised to finish the first half of league play on top. We ultimately met the season's second half winner to compete for a league championship. It was like reaching the Super Bowl. Our opponent team was aptly named The Destroyers and that's usually what they did to most competition. They were anchored by a rugged gal who looked like a football linebacker. Don't worry, I told my teammates, we're all going to receive at least second place trophies. Mother and several other parents came to cheer us on. Well, our opponents lived up to their reputation and each of us received a special second place trophy. I proudly set mine on a shelf of fresh made memories as a five gallon smile poured through.

The natural beauty of Red Rock Canyon caressed my heart and kissed my soul at a tender time of life. Rising majestically beyond the Las Vegas Valley, a geologic rainbow of sandstone glory blesses all who receive her. Soft pink and vibrant red flow through rivers of rock as sunlit gold and perfect blue adorn each mountain top. The first time I discovered that jeweled vista was on a weekend drive with dad. Let's go see Red Rock, he called, as we boarded the U.S.S. Chevy. We rose above some rocky waves and passed through mountain moors, then glanced along some sandstone bergs to reach our desert shores. Dad celebrated our successful arrival with a cold cream soda. Mother embraced a chilled can of Cactus Cooler as we younger shipmates disembarked with our own Shasta sodas.

Dad hoisted his bronze metal detector from the worn pickup bed. We dreamt of silver dollars and golden nuggets too, then followed on a broken trail where wagons once passed through. The detector moaned and briefly wailed as we leaned to quickly dig. I searched the soil and moved some rock, then raised an iron lid. We had discovered a large cache of bent bottle caps. I lifted the desert doubloons in both hands and realized we were already rich. Linda found a fresh batch of pollywogs and tiny frogs swimming in a desert stream. She scooped them into a cookie jar, studied them thoroughly and became Darwin for a day. I came upon some sandstone marbles that lay for untold days. They patiently sat on bedrock floors just waiting for someone to play. Phyllis found a bright cactus in bloom and treasured the colors it gave. The sun just seemed to smile as it wrapped our Red Rock day and Rainbow Peak was glowing with amber golden rays.

I returned to Red Rock Canyon many times in my youth. A friend and I once rode our ten speed bikes there on a wondrous journey. We cycled all the way to a panoramic summit and beyond, where skyward colors touched the land, to a place where rainbows began.

Fruits Of Our Labor

Some folks are good at math while others like to sing. A few may dance upon the moon as others watch and dream. Dad seemed to just have a knack for designing and building things, especially homes. If pops had lived in prehistoric time, his cave would have been the most functional and fuel efficient on the block or perhaps the entire mountainside. Our small home at Indian Springs was born through his thrifty plans and determined hands. The durable A-frame cabin dad crafted for us in Lee Canyon was an engineering marvel of 1963. The custom rockwork and walkways around our El Camino home in Las Vegas were signatures of his creative design process. Watermills of inspiration were often moving in dad's mind as fresh buckets splashed forth upon a thirsty drawing table. Detailed sketches of a unique H-shaped Spanish style home began to emerge and multiply like rabbits. Everyone would have their own room and we could ride the crest of modern technology through the incredible 70's and beyond.

I was quickly appointed deputy director in our new department of labor. My salary of $1 per hour also included a generous supply of Big Macs and fries while at the job site. As you know, fringe benefits are sometimes the best part of an employment package. We broke ground in 1972 as I plunged my well-worn shovel into a fresh desert palette. Dad squinted as he peered through a small surveyor's glass while I held the measuring rod steady. We checked, rechecked and staked the lot to perfection. When building a home, it's good to begin in the right place. I was mighty glad when a large road grader showed up to level the lot. Now we had round point, square point and even long point shovels. I guess the real point is that you could move a lot more dirt with a grader than with a shovel and still enjoy a lemonade during the process. Once level with the globe, I gave the ground a good watering to help it settle. A mammoth gravel truck arrived just a few days later, brimming with #2 rock fill. I didn't realize that rocks had numbers, but they do. I moved a few thousand of them around the lot to build up a strong foundational pad for the concrete slab.

Mother kept a vital McDonald's supply train rolling and her lunchtime arrivals were most welcome. The Coleman ice jug was frequently filled and I drank enough of the life-giving water to actually lower Lake Mead. Trenches were dug squarely along foundational perimeters and I became proud of my burrowing abilities. Dad showed me how to set rebar stakes within each trench footer and tie in great lengths of steel for strength. Each prepared trench would then be filled with fresh cement and become strong enough to support the corners, walls and roof of a solid home. Shovels, wheelbarrows, sledgehammers and steel had all helped forge an iron grip within twelve year old hands. We set and staked forms for the foundation as rough plumbing was then complete. Every detail was ready for the all-important pour.

Cement trucks arrived early that morning and our crew was fully equipped with every tool of their hard rock trade. They poured a splendid single layer cake of delicious cement mixed with crunchy granola gravel. Every team member had a special routine as they danced in the concrete mud. Some screened the mixture with long wooden forms while others tamped and troweled. They also gathered loose gelatin into pools of delectable chowder. Finishers buffed the mellow grey and gave it a glossy sheen. Anchor bolts lined each sweetened edge and topped our pistachio dream. I spread a light mist of water across the surface to give it some added strength. A brief rainbow appeared in the cooling spray as it touched a new foundation that day. A drop of sweat then kissed a stone as we gently smiled and traveled home.

There's something special about a fresh bundle of Boise Cascade lumber. The scent of sawmills and evergreen forests brought our desert homesite to life. Progress accelerated as each framed wall was lifted. Portals for doorways and windows quickly appeared with each new day of accomplishment. A symphony of electric skilsaws surrounded us as steady hammers drummed in time. I also added a few two-by-fours in good measure. The roof was a crowning event as thick sheets of plywood protected us from the elements. Newly installed windows and doors brought a closer sense of home. Mesh lath paper then wrapped our developing home which temporarily resembled a large chicken coop. The stucco scratch coat and subsequent second layer brought our emerging home ever closer to the beautiful butterfly stage. A sunrise yellow color coat then flowed upon it all like the breath of life.

Dad and I ran enough electrical wire through that house to light up a city stadium. He marked each wood stud as I drilled quarter-size holes for the vital cable. I flipped and hammered more electrical boxes than pancakes in every room and hallway. Dad showed me how to install outlet plugs and light switches which I did throughout the house. I also helped run and cut wire while connecting and stapling it securely in place. We ended up with almost as many power outlets as politicians, but ours were more reliable and cost a lot less. Now Mario was an exceptional finish carpenter and completed our cabinetry, pantry, door trim and baseboards. He came to us with a song in his heart from Italy and everyone loved him. Mario and I enjoyed each day as we talked of many fine things and labored together.

Home insulation was our next project and I stapled what seemed like endless rolls of it in the ceiling and sidewalls. I was glad to see it covered with sheetrock and watched as strong men struggled to lift and secure the massive gypsum boards. Every corner, joint and dimple was covered with finishing tape and compound. I filled and sanded every scar as if restoring a favorite car. Ceilings and walls then received a complete textured caress. Everyone pitched in with painting and we colored our world anew. Many days and several nights were spent romancing a paint brush, roller and pan. A bright display of radiant light and crystal swag lamps adorned our fresh new home. Harvest gold carpet covered many rooms and chocolate shag my own.

We moved in a few days before Christmas and sat down to rest in some comfortable bean bag chairs. Our cat Peter carefully explored his new digs and gave a hearty meow of approval.

We made it, dad quietly declared.

Mother nodded with a full smile as she set a fresh platter of delicious fruit on the table.

The house we built together served us for many seasons and soon became a place we gladly called home.

Alberta and Joe were good family friends and as good a people as you could find. Through the years, we enjoyed flame roasted meals and warm times around the glowing campfires of Lee Canyon. Dad and Joe had become well acquainted through their work in health physics at the Nevada Test Site. Joe looked a lot like President Dwight Eisenhower and was rather bright to match. He liked to tinker with things and once assembled an entire working airplane as a hobby project. Dad and Joe often talked about scientific theories while visiting for hours. Together they sailed through time and space till one of them had to go home.

Donnie, I'm going to see Joe and Alberta for a while, do you want to come along?

You and Dean can do some fun things together while we talk.

Dean was their youngest son and we were both about the same age.

Sure dad, I'll go with you.

Alberta welcomed us in as she called to Dean.

Donnie's here, why don't you show him your record player while Jay and Joe talk at the table.

As we listened to some of Dean's 45 rpm records, one tune especially held my attention.

I really like that one, can we hear it again?

"Close to You," sung by The Carpenters, was a beautiful melody and the words uplifting. The more I listened to each flowing verse, the more beautiful it became. I played that record at least twenty times and wondered which girl I could kiss as she and I grew together in love. Perhaps some music is just born beautiful. When we got home that night, I told mother of a wonderful song just discovered and wanted to hear more of that sweet music from the Carpenters.

As you can guess, dad liked to design and build things. Lumber, electrical wire, concrete and rebar, these were materials that could transform blueprint designs into physical reality. A good labor source was also needed, which often included me. We soon heard about a good deal on some previously salvaged building materials from the

Test Site. Like Mel Fisher, we were in search of untold treasure. These great finds lay not off coastal shores, but along parched and dusty desert floors. All we needed was a large enough truck to haul the dinosaur relics home. Dad borrowed a behemoth old flatbed for the desert voyage. It appeared to have once rolled with Patton's 3rd Army. I inquired of dad if the ol boy had enough drive left in the tank to get us there and back.

I think so, he said with a hopeful yet concerned look. We just need it for a day.

Also, Joe called and said Dean would like to come. You two should have plenty to talk about along the way.

Mother prepared some classic sandwiches as we filled the Coleman ice chest, water jug and truck. She then waived as if we were going off to war. A funny feeling rattled my twelve year old bones as the fossil flatbed lurched forward. Could we make it across the sun-scorched desert? Lathrop Wells was about 90 slow miles from Las Vegas and it didn't take long for Dean and I to tap into some luxurious sandwiches and cold 7-Up. Somewhere beyond Indian Springs, an old dashboard needle gauge began to dance. By the time we made Mercury, it leaned steadily towards H. Did the bright red H stand for hot or hell? With oven roasting temperatures it was really hard to tell. How much further to our blessed destination? On we drove as Dean and I downed a couple more root beers. Waves of radiant heat rose from the highway as oxygen seemed to evaporate from the air. Finally, Lathrop Wells began to appear on a bleak horizon. It looked like the last stop between here and the moon, but right about then was welcome indeed.

A cloud of powdered dust rose as we pulled into the remote station. The lumbering truck sighed with a long breath of steam as it stopped. We carefully lifted the large round hood as water continued to trickle and vaporize upon a skillet like engine. A grizzled sun worn fellow then emerged from the roadside station as we closely inspected the overheated truck. Yep, a cracked engine block, not much we could do. The whole motor would need to be rebuilt and the nearest mechanics for that job were back in Las Vegas. Well, the truck still ran and everyone decided it was best to try and make it back to town. We filled every container we had with water as the engine simmered and cooled. The nice station man had a life-saving pop machine and we gave it a month's worth of business in just a day. The red and white refrigerated cooler held thick green bottles of Coke, Nehi Orange and a rack of frosty root beer – an excellent menu. We thoroughly filled an onboard ice chest and also ourselves.

A couple calls were made to concerned mothers and we assured them of our eventual return. The trip would be dicey and weather was crucial. Like sailing The Horn of Africa, we calculated temperatures and time of day, then set forth on our return voyage. We pointed the tired truck towards home and shook hands with the kind station man who wished us well. I held watch on the odometer and counted each long mile as we rumbled forward. We made ten miles before the temperature gauge became frozen on hot as billowing steam vented from Mount Hood. After cooling for several minutes, I placed a towel over the refried radiator cap, gently turned it and jumped for cover. Precious water was then poured in and on we drove for twelve more miles. Lather, rinse, repeat. We gained eighteen additional miles before all the water ran out. After 40 miles, there was no more water for the cooling system.

Please help us make it, I silently prayed. We all need to get back home.

What should we do?

The engine needs to be rebuilt anyway, dad said.

How much soda pop do we have?

We've got several bottles of 7-Up, cola and root beer, I declared.

Alright, when it cools enough, pour in the 7-Up first, he instructed.

The thirsty truck gulped five bottles of 7-Up and was satisfied for nine more miles as sweet syrup drizzled from the hood.

We're going to make it, I boldly told my troops.

By then, I had become rather efficient at removing the half-baked radiator cap. In went the cola and on we rolled. A couple more stops after sundown brought us ever closer to salvation. We had four bottles of root beer left and twelve miles to go. A frothy foam bubbled as I poured it all in. The old radiator belched again as I tightened the cap once more. A half hour later, we chugged into town and then on home. A front porch lamp beckoned us and seemed brighter than a lighthouse beacon. That night, home really was sweet home.

About two weeks later the phone rang and dad answered in the kitchen.

Oh no! I'm so sorry, he uttered.

Is there anything we can do?

There was a somber stillness as he released the phone. Mother quickly asked dad what had happened.

There's been an accident. Dean was struck by a car today and died.

Mother began to cry. She held me close and could hardly speak.

I lay awake for a long time that night. It almost didn't seem real.

I'm sorry for what happened to you, I whispered.

If you can hear me Dean, what's it like in heaven?

Sometime later, Joe and Alberta came over to visit. Everyone sat together in the living room as Alberta reached to hold my hand. Her eyes were moist and her arm began to tremble. My heart wept for her and Joe. How difficult it must be to lose someone you love…someone close to you.

Now I believe that good things can always grow with enough loving care and we gave a lot of it to almost everything we planted. Dad chose two majestic olive trees to keep watch in our new front yard. All we needed was a pair of colossal hand dug holes to help them feel welcome. I had already received an advanced degree in digging from the prestigious School of Hard Work. There I majored in earth removal sciences with an emphasis on shovel and wheelbarrow physics. My postgraduate studies included extensive labor in the transportation of geologic material with a special focus on theories of lumbar recovery. So, dad carved a wide arc across some barren ground and asked if I was ready for the great challenge. My sun gilt hand grasped his with confidence as I received the staff of an ancient shovel in the other.

You're going to find solid caliche and will need to break through it, he instructed.

The large trees can only flourish with ample room for the roots to reach beyond that thick rock barrier.

Of course, why I could dig through the Rocky Mountains if need be. Dad then presented me with a five foot wedged iron bar. The javelin like tool was really a manual jackhammer without an electric cord. I was the power source and determination the fuel. Now I'm convinced that caliche didn't come from the Garden of Eden. It's tough as cement and stronger than stone. For three days I swung a pick, lifted shovels and raised a mighty mound of earth. Mother brought me refreshing tumblers of cold lemonade to help wash the dust down. Well, even before Rocky Balboa, I went round after round pounding away at a bruising opponent. I swung hard from the left and countered to the right as blue sparks leapt from iron and caliche collisions. My body leaned and wavered with exhaustion.

Please God, help me get through the solid rock to better ground.

In that moment, I heard calm yet profound words of inspiration – "Keep Digging."

I did and two hours later broke through to find the soft soil of Eden. Dad and I carefully moved the great trees into their new place and surrounded them with a nourishing blend of good earth. Mother gave the thirsty trees a steady supply of cool water as they settled in for about 30 years or more. Those peaceful trees brought forth a continuous bounty of olives as grateful birds shared in the abundant harvest. It seemed there was always more fruit than our baskets could bear.

Mother and dad were often partial to palm trees and we selected several to join our desert oasis on Lindell Road. They grew as we did and stoutly weathered the winds of time. Now Italian cypress are kind of like angels and seemed to follow us since early childhood. We posted several of the stately sentinels around our yard and they stood tall in every season. Arborvitaes were also a favorite and we cared for them all as dear friends. Our cat Peter especially enjoyed wiggling his tender nose among their fragrant branches. The almond trees we planted blossomed early each year and were the first to celebrate a coming new spring. Mother cared for the lovely trees as each summer harvest filled baskets of plenty.

My favorite was the Aleppo pine tree I brought home in a half gallon bucket. The little Charlie Brown tree spoke to me at a Grand Central store, so I bought it for $1.69. I gently touched the soft green branches and just knew it had to be mine. Mother also admired the little fellow and asked where I wanted to plant my new tree. I quietly walked around the entire yard and carefully considered each possible place while consulting the tiny tree. Together we chose a special place and it just felt right. I dug a beautiful two by three foot hole and filled it with every good thing a new tree could love. Peter watched as I set the sapling among fertile soil that sunny President's Day.

Dear God, please help my small tree live and grow well.

Come see the new tree, I urged while leading mother along.

Isn't it beautiful?

Yes Donnie, make sure you give it enough water.

Oh, I will…and water it I did.

The little pine tree quickly grew a foot, just like me, and then another. I visited my little tree in good times and when sad, touched each branch with grateful hands and pinecones in the sand. I whispered heartfelt words of love for all the evergreen, it swayed so ever gently and sang them back to me. It reached above the housetop high, to open skies beyond. Then leaned to touch my weary arm and bid me to be strong.

A warm and watchful sun is the keeper of every good crop and we always got plenty of it in Nevada. Since the ol boy was already smiling on most of the southwest, I asked if he could send enough life-giving rays to help our new garden grow. His reply was a generous 105 with buckets of warmth to spare. Perhaps the organic idea for a fresh garden sprang through Mimi and Grandad, whose Texas farming roots ran for generations. Mother received a cheerful photo of Mimi standing in her garden alongside a three foot zucchini she had grown. Her smile was wide as the Pecos River and I realized they really did grow things bigger in Texas. I decided to climb aboard that wagon and become farmer Don in the desert.

Our dry parcel wasn't always gentle and green like those of Texas or Tennessee. In fact, it had been left in a microwave far too long. My plan was to dig a square plot by the side of our house and fill it with mulchy sand. I labored all day and prepared a soft bed of ready-made land.

What should we plant? I eagerly asked mother.

Green beans might be good.

I traveled to Vegas Village and followed my nose to the fragrant garden department. A deep display of colorful seed packets presented themselves to wandering shoppers. I focused on the green bean offerings and shook each package near my ear. Now this was the golden age of written instruction and even garden seeds came with a how to guide. I tenderly planted each seed of promise in my blessed garden and promptly explained to Peter that it wasn't a special cat box. Each day I watered the furrowed land and thanked the sun above. When would our seeds break forth, embraced by so much love? About eight days later, the ground lifted as gorgeous green appeared. I shared the glad news with everyone and felt a curious bond with each new sprout. Our beanstalks grew quickly, though not quite to the sky and made some tasty beans on the very first try.

What else could we grow?

Dad thought red radishes were vogue. I gathered a group of the mighty seeds, plowed them in and made it so.

Try this one dad, how does it taste?

Like a radish, he laughed.

Let's try something sweeter, we agreed.

A classic melon would be sweet indeed. Sugar baby watermelons sure seemed good, so I planted more seeds, as many as we could. Pretty yellow blossoms clung to fast growing vines as I nourished them with Lake Mead's finest water. Mother and I waded through an ever-expanding jungle of thriving vines as more melons appeared each day. I encouraged and listened to each growing fruit and thus became the watermelon whisperer. Our small garden produced an incredible 200 sugar baby watermelons that season. It took an extra patio fridge just to hold them all. Someone planted a couple surprise seeds in our garden and I nourished them as well. Two small sprouts became a pair of hearty pumpkin vines. Brilliant star-shaped blossoms burst forth on the vines which grew to 45 feet in length. Vivid orange pumpkins brought added joy to an abundant and colorful harvest. I sat with mother among our enchanted garden patch and exclaimed in endless laughter, "Oh Great Pumpkin! When are You coming back?"

Everyone can plant a garden filled with special dreams. Just nourish it with careful love and watch the fruit it brings.

Fishing For Rainbows

My thirteenth year opened with a treasure chest of sparkling experience as each new season revealed more to come. Now dad once sailed the pacific blue and fished a few days in the gem of his youth. Thirsty lake waters still glistened nearby as they beckoned and tickled the shores of his mind. It wasn't long before a trio of hungry Zebco rod and reels landed in our living room. Dad also gave me a Bible – The Fisherman's Bible, which I faithfully turned to for outdoor inspiration. Tales of fisherman finding their nirvana in remote rivers and streams, soon swept me away in day drifting dreams.

The once peaceful fishing aisles at Woolco now lured me in for a feeding frenzy. I gobbled up salmon eggs on sale, jars of fresh garlic cheese bait, rainbow colored marshmallows and juicy plastic worms. Choosing a tackle box was almost like buying a new car. There were so many models and features. Should I purchase a two drawer or four drawer, compact or deluxe edition? Dad suggested we carry a large net to help land our future quarry. The one we chose appeared deep enough to lift even Nessie ashore. Vegas Village also carried a deep array of tackle in their fishing bay. My favorite lure was a purple and white shad which I still treasure today. Mother completed our fishing dream team as we set forth on a journey to Lake Mead.

Our first fishing trip was shortly after New Year's Day 1974, following a record snowfall in Las Vegas, the most since 1949. We stepped aboard the old Chevy truck which seemed to live forever and scooted through the crunchy snow like a ski patrol on wheels. Lake Mead appeared sleepy that day as we carried our camp to shore. Mother's first cast flew just seven feet and mine about four. Dad showed us all how it was done and proceeded to hook the largest bush near shore. If catching our dinner was vital, we'd better head for the nearest drive-through and fast. Fortunately, after several more casts we were fishing like pros.

Mother, have you ever gone fishing before?

When I was about five, living on the farm with Mother and Daddy, we had a horse tank. I tied an open metal clothespin to a string and wrapped it around a stick pole. I held my line in that horse tank for a long time and felt sure to catch something.

Did you?

No, but sure thought I would.

Well mother, Lake Mead is bigger than a horse tank and your chances look better today.

Ok, we didn't catch anything that first brisk fishing day, but the excitement of trying kept us warm. On the way home, I gave dad a quiz.

How many fish do you think are really in Lake Mead?

Not sure, he replied.

Let's come back and find out, I laughed, and give it another try.

Lake Mead quickly became a best friend that I eagerly looked forward to seeing again. I checked my tackle box one more time before setting the alarm clock for our predawn departure. A fisherman's wake up call comes early and we soon saddled up. Even the old truck had waited all week for another fishing trip and seemed most happy with us in it. The sun was yet to crest an early horizon as we rolled near the Ye Ol Fishin Hole bait store on Boulder Highway. Some say it had been there since the 1940s and a dangling string of ancient bells tried to jingle as we entered inside. A full bearded fellow with sleep in his eyes and a molten cup of coffee sprang from a momentary slumber to greet us. He appeared to have sailed the Seven Seas for many years and was just glad to be home.

My son and I are headed to the lake. What kind of bait do you recommend we bring?

What are you fishing for? the bait shop captain replied.

Trout, bass – whatever's biting I guess.

Got some real nice Canadian nightcrawlers, just came in.

He lifted a styrofoam lid to reveal twelve plump wigglers ready for action.

Sold, we'll take two fresh cartons.

How bout some lively minnows?

A sweet aroma then rose as he opened a mysterious bait tank.

Which ones are the best? I asked.

Oh, they're all pretty good, he assured me.

Upon closer inspection, I noticed a few were floating on their side and didn't look so well.

Which would you rather eat, a live minnow or dead one, I wondered.

Our friend also highlighted a special jar of salmon eggs which held great potential, so we corralled that too. As we thanked our wise guide and reboarded the pickup, I gazed back to see the kind store captain drifting away in his sailing chair … to fond places distant and times without care.

Some early morning lights of Boulder City still twinkled as we rounded a bend before dawn. The miracle of a new day was enough to lighten any load and lift us along the way. Hemenway Harbor soon appeared and framed that new day. We followed a beautiful dirt road where only fishermen or someone lost might go. Unloading our gaggle of fishing gear was a bit noisy. Be quiet and don't scare the fish, dad kept reminding me. We stealthily made our way along a secret shore much like the Pink Panther when searching for clues.

Here! dad whispered at the point of a rocky hill.

I searched the carton of worms for a frisky volunteer and placed the lucky fellow on my hook with a sweet marshmallow. I launched the sumptuous offering northward, as if casting towards Canada and waited with measured patience. The best pole holders are often found among natural rocks and I gathered a few for the day.

Please God, help us catch a good fish and have a nice day too.

Some time later, I noticed my reel handle turning.

Look dad!

Gently pick it up and let the fish take more line, he instructed.

Now set the hook, but not too hard.

The pole bent forward as something pulled even more.

It's a good fish, keep reeling but don't try to horse it in, he continued.

I decided to let dad enjoy some fun and offered him the rod of glory. He excitedly reeled as we scanned the water for a glimpse of our first fish. A silvery shadow drew near as I reached for the net.

Head first Donald, scoop the fish head first so it stays in the net.

It's a big rainbow trout, he exclaimed.

Sunlight shimmered along a pink and green bow set in sparkling silver. The beautiful 3 ½ pound trout swam to our net and into my heart. Dad also caught a small pan-size trout before the sunset circled a perfect day. I guess you really can touch rainbows and our Coleman ice chest held two of them. Mother made some forever photos of dad and I holding our first fish. We named the great trout Charlie and baked it for a special feast. I still see him swimming in waters so clear with memories of gladness that flow through the years.

Our first fishing boat was a brave twelve foot skiff that came to us from pastures unknown. It wasn't really made for the deep waters of Lake Mead and thank goodness for a handy bailing bucket. Dad bought the small boat for a song and we labored diligently to bring it seaworthy. Having served in the Navy, dad followed maritime protocol and gave me clear instructions to Scrub the deck Matey! We outfitted her with a dependable 3.5 horsepower trolling motor and I was promoted to chief fuel engineer. This meant I could mix and carry all fuel tanks. I also operated the ship's horn which was frequently tested. Bright orange seemed to be a suave color of the day and we soon sported matching life vests. I quickly found a regal captain's hat that fit my large head well. If dad took a convenient snooze on board, I promptly wore it and assumed temporary command.

We officially launched the mighty vessel at Hemenway Harbor with an attending crowd of four. I ceremoniously christened her with a frosty can of A&W root beer after enjoying a hearty first gulp myself. We sailed for a nearby island just this side of the Galapagos and discovered a natural cove teeming with bluegill. We fished the pristine waters of paradise and gnawed upon succulent fried chicken that mother made for our voyage. After drifting with the sun for a few more hours, we surfed on a trade wind and glided for home. I returned that day to welcome shores with salty tales of sailing lore. Our quest had found horizon's end, where songbirds sing and dreams ascend.

Dad soon heard of a new place to fish and suggested we follow an old glory trail along El Dorado Canyon. Nelson's Landing lay several miles below Hoover Dam on the scenic Colorado River. Some call it Lake Mohave, but to me, she'll always be the river. A narrow yet inviting road led from the small town of Nelson toward a waiting river of destiny. I heard the whispering hills of El Dorado had untold tales to tell. I cranked open a window, tilted my ear and listened for many a spell. Roughshod miners once followed a dream of riches, fortune and fame. While some found gold in pockets of ore, others found dust and dry rain.

Now launching the boat always brought a few brief moments of focus. I loosened the bow winch, removed trailer tie downs and wrangled with a limited tow line. Dad backed the trailer in till our truck exhaust gurgled in the river, then quickly hit the brakes. If all went well, the happy boat left the trailer and I reeled it in with my rope. I displayed a multitude of creative hand signals as dad peered with puzzled looks in the side view mirror. Go left, now right, keep coming, slow down, go again, now stop! For a few moments, I really had him in the palm of my hand. One morning, the boat got too excited upon launch and got away. I swiftly ran down a wobbly dock and caught the rope just in time, before it drifted on towards Argentina.

Dad often scanned a blue and beige horizon as I steered the loyal ship. A few hidden coves near Nelson easily became our favorite destination. We invited Sam and his dad to join us there for a sunny day of fishing that still shines. Upon reaching our cove of splendor, I tied the boat to a riverside tree. Now trout have good taste and often prefer cheese. Whether Swiss, American or Smokey Cheddar, they're fairly easy to please. That fresh block of Velveeta was a fisherman's bar of gold and we were always wealthy. It's the one kind of bait you can eat with crackers if the fish don't bite. Well, they sure nibbled my cheese that day and I landed five gorgeous rainbows before we sailed away.

Mother returned with us to that special fishing cove, amid endless tales of trout, swimming in glory and gold. She hoped to also catch a pan size trout and patiently held her reel. I encouraged and cheered her on for nibbles that she could feel.

Keep trying mother, there's a nice one out there just for you.

Thirty minutes later, her date arrived and oh, what a great surprise.

Something's really on here, she hollered.

Keep reeling mother, nice and steady.

He's too big, she gasped.

Let him run a little, you're doing fine. I'm right here with the net when you're ready.

Well, that fish swam like Mark Spitz and covered almost every point on a compass. The epic event was fully crowned as we raised a glistening four pound rainbow from the water.

That's a lot more than pan size, dad said with surprise.

What a fish mother, you did it!

She sat wide-eyed and out of breath for several moments.

A radiant smile then lit her face, a touch of gold in every place.

You see, the hills of El Dorado still sparkle today,

In deep canyons of memory and rich rivers of jade.

Now dad decided to get a slightly larger boat so we could go more places on the lake. We weren't trying to keep up with the Joneses because they didn't have a boat. Besides, ours were from the 60s and not exactly showroom quality. If it didn't sink, we were happy. A fourteen foot navy blue boat with deep hull and outboard motor opened the way west. Dual gas tanks from another era kept our thirsty motor roaring. You really don't want to run out of gas this side of Barstow with no station in sight. Fishing ski raft cove was now a snap and the intake tower too. Like Columbus we sailed for distant lands across a deeper blue. Black Canyon and Hoover Dam were some of the furthest points west on Lake Mead. We gathered supplies and charted our course for a journey of great discovery.

Lake Mead water levels were high back then and many tempting coves lured us along the way. Yet fishing our lines near the dam was the ultimate place of choice. I quickly discovered that sunset to dawn was the best biting time for fish and mosquitos. The green Coleman lantern which illuminated our Lee Canyon cabin on so many winter nights, now turned the darkness of Black Canyon bright. We spent many nights on the water gazing at the vast heavens above and wondering of the unknown depths below. Glasslike waters reach out for as long as the moonlight accepts them. Night birds keep time as big rigs gear down over the dam, sending echoes through the canyon. A seal beam sways slowly as the boat moves to reveal an astronomical panorama of stars, planets and galaxies. Thousands of neon blue fry dart beneath our light in their brief moments of ecstasy. Eternity is interrupted momentarily as a searching catfish strikes my bait. Even the mosquitos find a temporary home in the exquisite light of our lantern.

Sleepy skies begin to turn light blue over the mountains which appear as a rough sketch. Small animals rustle along the shoreline as they sense a new morning approach. The whole world begins to soak up color and take form. Creation is in its dawn and light flickering stars fade slowly away. A lone night bird remains, hoping to escape the morning with his song, but soon realizes that he too must retreat, for the night has given way.

Now dad heard that large trout went to school at night in the deep waters of Black Canyon. We decided to attend class with them and invite a lucky few to join us for a special cooking seminar. Several three to five pound rainbow trout accepted and were warmly treated at a delicious event hosted by mother. It's true, sometimes you can find colorful rainbows even at night.

We didn't go fishing every week because dad's sketch pad just couldn't rest. He designed a new workshop and carport surrounded by walkways and cinder block walls. Just guess who helped him build it all. I hammered more nails, painted more wood and mixed more concrete than a full-time construction crew. By the age of fourteen, I wore thick calluses across both hands that were tougher than a Texas Longhorn. The excitement of every new fishing trip was welcome indeed as a rod, reel and tackle box stood ready to set me free.

The boat was almost ready as I packed our gear and filled the ice chest onboard. Mother made a variety of tasty sandwiches for a full day at the river. I wore my favorite windbreaker, a light blue jacket with colorful trout and bass patches on each shoulder. Mother had also sewn a special name patch on the front. Our destination that day was a familiar one – Nelson's Landing. We were well prepared and ready when dad suddenly stared at me in the carport. An odd look came upon his now furrowed face.

Donald, your hair's too long. We're not going till you get a haircut.

Today? I muttered in confusion.

Yes, we're not leaving till you go get a haircut, he insisted.

This was going to delay our happy departure and cause us to arrive much later at Nelson.

Mother, I don't know why dad keeps yacking about my hair.

Could you please drive me to the haircut place so we can get going?

The fish don't care how long my hair is, I grumbled.

Well, after a considerable delay, we finally got under way.

That's better, dad smiled, as he approved of my new coiffure.

Now we can go.

As we turned south from Boulder Highway, dark clouds hovered in the distance.

Looks like it might be raining over at Nelson, dad observed.

Maybe, but fish can be active during a good sprinkle, I replied.

It could be storming by the river, he motioned.

We hadn't really noticed, but no vehicles from the other direction had even passed by since we turned on the road to Nelson. As we reached the rustic town, about five miles above the landing, rocky debris lay strewn along the road. A frantic woman rushed from her home and scrambled across soggy ground. She waved her arms wildly as we stopped to help.

It's gone! she blurted with trembling lips.

It's not there anymore!

What happened?

It's all gone, she cried.

You won't be able to get through.

We then saw that portions of the road ahead had vanished. There must have been a flash flood in the surrounding hills and canyon below. Just then, someone on a motorcycle came racing by as if he'd seen a ghost. A short time later, emergency vehicles, search and rescue teams, news coverage and helicopters came streaming in from Las Vegas. Survivors of the mega flash flood that swept through El Dorado Canyon and Nelson's Landing on September 14, 1974, estimated the wall of water to have been 20 to 40 feet high. Dad's unexplained notion for me to get a haircut had spared us from great peril. Perhaps a still small voice we sometimes hear had saved and kept us well.

Dad decided to get a bigger boat to hold all those fish we were catching. He found a shy sixteen foot cabin cruiser at the boat pound that just needed a little love. Well, what it really needed was unconditional love. You see, the boat had been underwater for two weeks following a storm at Lake Mead. It was the ultimate fixer-upper.

Donald, I found a good boat that needs some work.

We can restore it and have a nice boat for fishing.

I'll need your help.

Sure dad.

I was promoted to first officer as we shook hands.

Over the months, we removed, sanded and varnished each piece of wood trim anew. Glass windows were cut for the top and side ports for us to clearly see through. Engine and tanks were rebuilt and restored so they ran just the same as when new. We covered the deck and bow of our boat with a gorgeous aqua blue. Wheel and cables were fitted to spin and move with the agile crew. She ran like a top and glowed like a gem as we polished each curve to brand new. It truly was a bright day as we placed fresh letters and numbers on the bow of our ship. Mother had seen our great effort and we all smiled stem to stern.

Let's give our new boat a name, I announced at the dinner table.

Dad reflected as if gazing toward the Great Lakes and beyond.

Let's call it Second Chance, I suggested.

Mother liked the name and dad did too. Even the boat wiggled its flag with hearty approval.

It seems that some of the most beautiful boats are those we give a second chance.

Now dad didn't always hear so well as in those early years. Sam once asked him a deep question during one of our late night fishing tours.

Mr. Brady, are fish nocturnal?

What? dad replied.

Are fish like turtles??

We all laughed as Sam repeated his question.

From that time forward, if anyone ever asked dad something he couldn't quite hear, his response was always the same – Are fish like turtles? It became code for I can't hear you.

One thing we all heard with each morning breeze was a call from the river and mighty Lake Mead. There were buckets of bluegill that swam in a shoal and peaceful reflections of Cathedral Cove. Echoing coyotes sang by the way as catfish and crappie swooned in the bay. The moonlight at Cottonwood on a silvery night, played a sonata gentle and bright. Bacon and eggs on a sunrise shore, welcomed my morning and journey du jour. We fished more nights at Willow Beach on the Arizona bend of the river than were stars that watched above. I guess the great lake and ever flowing river accepted me and I found myself in them. So, when cares of the world swirled about and sorrow touched my hand, I went in search of rainbows and always found a friend.

Passages Of Time

Time is a gift given to all to share and spend as they may, from first born breath to angel steps in the sweet golden light of day. Waking up to a new school year was nice but sleeping still felt better. The warmth of summer waved goodbye as an early autumn whispered. The blessing of getting us to school now rested upon Phyllis. Somehow, dad bought a hapless car that already needed CPR. My aviator glasses weren't always clean, but I could clearly see the car we would ride to school in was a certified clunker. Phyllis was the lucky recipient of said Rambler that was born to be in a junkyard.

Now Phyllis was pretty and we cheered as she participated in the Nevada Junior Miss Pageant of 1973. Her jazz and tap dancing skills were sweet as she garnered first place for poise and an appearance in the finals. The ramblin wreck she drove for a time just didn.t seem fitting. Our journey to school each morning became an episode of laughter and uncertainty. Getting the reluctant car to start was our first goal. If successful, we bobbled forward amid silent prayers of petition and thanksgiving.

Please God, don't let the car die before we get to school.

I often pulled on the front passenger door to keep it closed during rolling right turns. The stoic Rambler also had a chronic case of vapor lock and frequently died in traffic. Some drivers honked like noisy geese while a few helped push our ripe lemon toward a roadside rest. A normal ten minute trip to school could take half an hour. Phyllis eventually got a better car and we waved a cheerful goodbye to the old Rambler that tried. We also rescued an avocado green Ranchero that could only have lived in the 70s. I drove it around the yard like a tractor hauling sand and other building materials.

A driver's education class was offered during my sophomore year of high school. The instructor asked if I was familiar with how to operate a vehicle.

Some, I replied.

Following a few hours of after school instruction, Pat invited each student to sit behind the wheel. Let's see how you do with orange cones around a parking lot course. Some kids lurched forward as others made wild figure eight turns. He seemed surprised as I maneuvered through the course with easy acceleration, handling and brakes.

Really good Don, have you ever driven before?

Well, here and there, since about age ten.

During the last week of class, Pat accompanied each of us on a student drive to Red Rock Canyon. I carefully followed his instructions as if navigating a desert slalom course.

Fine Don, just fine. Let's turn around and head back to town.

I guess Pat was comfortable and somewhat tired from a full day as he soon drifted off to peaceful pastures. I didn't want to wake him and thought it wonderful if we could make it back to town and the high school before he awoke. I accelerated gently and went easy on the brakes as we cruised through traffic and intersections. About half way there, an abrupt snore woke Pat and he suddenly sat up. I just kept driving as he appeared surprised but also refreshed from the unexpected nap.

It was a happy day as mother and I stood in an eternal line at the hallowed Department of Motor Vehicles. At age 15 ½, I received a learner's permit to drive. Mother could now be my passenger as I gladly chauffeured her to the grocery store in a new world of Driving Miss Wanda. A few months later, I received my first solo driver's license and the keys to a beautiful brown Pinto. We were rollin and times were especially good.

Some of the most beautiful bells we'll ever hear will chime on wedding days. Phyllis heard them with joy on her twentieth birthday of 1976. Phyllis A. Brady and George A. McNeill made wonderful choices in giving their hearts to each other. The roads of life seem sweeter as we walk and run them together. Many celebrated the joyous proclamation that early summer day. Mimi and Grandad, Grandma Ann and Grandpa Earnie, Grandma Goforth, Mother and Dad and many more, all shared in a time of great gladness. The welcome bells of love we hear that sound on wedding days are more than just some chimes that ring and quickly fade away. Let's ring them every morning as sunrays rise to sing, like bluebirds in the summer time and blossoms of the spring.

If you ever find a little time in the breeze, the Great State of Texas is a fine place to be. In the summer of '76, I went to see Mimi and Grandad for a few splendid weeks. Now Amarillo is a pretty Spanish word for yellow. Mimi and Grandad drove a cool Ford LTD of the same color to match the city they now called home. We celebrated July 4th and America's Bicentennial watching fireworks and lighting a few of our own. I lit a lively string of firecrackers, turned to run and was met headfirst by a laughing lamppost. I don't know what it is about large objects and my tender noggin. Goalposts, diving boards, lampposts, they all seem attracted to my handsome head. Aunt Margie and Uncle June Barnhart then brought me to a festive red, white and blue rodeo. Almost everyone wore a great looking cowboy hat, even the young 'uns. Brahma bulls were jumpin for joy as each rider raised a hand to wave at the crowd. Well, I decided not to ride one of those happy bulls because of what might happen to my unlucky noggin.

Aunt Wilma and Uncle Harold Green invited me to their place for some of the best grilled burgers my mouth ever met. I'm convinced that Texas burgers are better engineered than any we ever had in Nevada. A new southwestern sun then brought Harold and Grandad's brother Raymond by with a full day of fishing for cousin Alan and I. Lake Meredith is an all-American dandy of the gentle Canadian River and we landed on soft golden shores of a sunfish stampede. Even the bluegill were bigger in Texas. My July fishing fever remained high as Mimi and Grandad took me to Southeast Lake in Amarillo for treatment. I found temporary relief wading through cool water and cattail groves in the splendor of summer afternoons. There I tracked a hungry herd of largemouth bass and cast colorful lures till my arm dropped with the sun. I returned from my great hunt on the open plains with full stringers of bass and bluegill. Still, every good fisherman needs plenty of practice, just like an ace pitcher with the Astros. One of my backyard practice casts sailed high over the plate and hooked a branch of Mimi's tallest tree. I believe that lure may still be there on Milam Street today, just waiting for a mighty bass to jump skyward and claim it.

Not far from the butter top plains of Amarillo is a geologic slice of Caprock cake that only God and time could make. Palo Duro

Canyon is the second largest canyon in America and a rich tapestry of Texas grandeur. Margie and June Barnhart along with Wilma and Harold Green lifted me to see a spectacular outdoor play held there each summer called TEXAS. Dramatic and inspiring scenes of Texas and her people flowed across a panoramic stage of natural beauty. A delicious BBQ sandwich had my taste buds also shouting – Encore!

As glorystars glittered in a Texas sky, I felt heaven near and understood why.

There are many great places a heart may roam, yet always in Texas you're closer to home.

The opening song of my sixteenth year flowed as an aria, rich and clear. Each new verse now wrapped in gold, touched by a sunrise soft and bold. I woke to the image of a faint mustache and Roman Brio in mirrored glass. I began to see the gladiator felt more often within. My new part-time job as a boxboy at Thriftimart was just a cover for my real identity. Each day after school, I faced a numerous host of fearless grocery carts in the parking lot arena. Some carried bent basket shields and others more seriously wounded wheels. Yet, I always showed mercy and ultimate care to the cheers of our emperor and customers there. The bright orange vest and black bow tie kept everyone apprised of my noble rank and status. Bagging groceries and serving others was a welcome rite of passage in this modern arena of life.

Now every bold warrior must face great challenge at times. I did as a clarion call echoed through the store–cleanup on aisle number four! Before me were the ruins of our leaning tower of pizza sauce display. 96 large jars of Ragu sauce lay broken and scattered across a stunned shoppers' battlefield. Oh, Mamma Mia! I followed thick trails of delicious pasta sauce from Parma to Palermo as my taste buds wept.

Yet, I cleaned and conquered and got the aisle swept. I was also elected to join a special operations team dedicated to product placement and appeal. Whatever you wanted, bacon, candy or cat litter – I knew each place and the very best deals.

Every night, I kept a clear eye on the time and was ever ready to make my premier announcement from a store microphone.

Attention customers: Thriftimart will be closing in 15 minutes. Please bring your items forward for a courteous checkout. We look forward to seeing you again and thanks for shopping at Thriftimart.

I performed various renditions of this for appreciative store audiences and like Sinatra, simply did it my way. I rounded up the last stray carts from a late night parking lot and herded them all in. The giant T shown brightly and then flickered dim. Time seemed to flow as Niagara Falls and appeared to never run dry. The seasons poured so quickly and rushed before our eyes.

Every man needs a good truck at some point in life and I believe sooner is better. Dad seemed to realize this and invited me to join in a special search for my first pickup. She needed a solid motor with low mileage and also to have been well cared for. Good looks were of course a plus. The '73 sky blue Chevy truck we found was sweeter than a double slice of German chocolate cake with marmalade on top. Everything about the pretty truck and camper shell just set well. Mother also thought it a special gem. Dad offered to let me pay for the truck through continued hard work and effort in time.

I installed off-road rims and tires which were popular in that day. Amber fog lamps crowned my truck's face with all-seeing eyes in the night. Colorful saddle blanket seat covers turned plain plaid fabric bright. A fancy new 8-track player had me singing with John Denver and Jim Croce at many crossroads and stoplights. My Midland CB radio helped me stay in touch with Houston Control as I drove through a vast and ever-changing universe. I don't know if someone can really love a truck, but I did mine. Bluegill, as I called her, traveled with me through mountains, rivers and valleys of time. Sam also had a truck and whatever one of us did, the other wasn't far behind.

I then bought an old twelve foot metal boat that we could haul in the back of my truck. We carried it to the backyard pool for a nautical test and set the merry boat afloat. The only problem was it didn't. That boat leaked like a porous bucket of politicians. I spent several days filling every seam with enough marine putty to drive a calm man nutty.

Please God, help me fix my boat so it doesn't sink.

Well, Old Ironsides finally sailed from my shipyard of hopeful repair and carried us onward in maritime glory.

Good friends are some of the greatest treasures you can find in life and I was glad to have met Bob. He lived just up the way from Sam on the same desert road. Bob was really smart, kind of like Einstein with hair to match. Well, mother sometimes called me Donzo. Sam heard it and did the same. Bob heard it and called me Dr. Zo. Thus, I received an honorary doctorate among friends where it really mattered most.

Hey Bob, Sam and I are taking my boat to the river on Saturday.

It'll be a lot of fun. Can you join us?

Sure, Dr. Zo.

Good, we'll come by about 4 am, see you then.

We arrived at Bob's place well before the sun did and tapped on his door. No response. We knocked a little more and could see a faint light within. I peered through the darkness and scrunched my nose against a window. There was Bob, sitting upright in a chair wearing his safari hat. He appeared to be in a state of unwakeable slumber.

How do we get him out?

I kept tapping while holding a one-way conversation with him through the door.

Bob, wake up.

Something finally roused him from a deep hibernation and he sprang from the chair.

A door opened as Bob found his bearing.

Did I miss it? he frantically wondered.

It's alright Bob, we're here to pick you up, you're fine.

A couple fresh maple bars were more effective than smelling salts and we were soon underway.

The Aztec Wash turn appeared at sunrise and we bounced along ten miles of gravel and washboard road towards the river. Upon arrival, we sailed the inside passage to a remote inlet and tranquil shores. There we swam with some panfish, warmed by a generous Mohave sun. As I crossed a serene turquoise cove and climbed ashore, a sharp rattle stopped me cold. An irritated snake was also enjoying some rays and not ready to give way. Bob was dog-paddling nearby with his glasses still on and headed for the same shore.

Rattlesnake! I yelled.

Go back, Bob!

Well, Bob instinctively dove down headfirst in the escape and came back up without his glasses. The cove was just too deep and we couldn't find them.

Look at it this way Bob, at least some fish out there can really see well now.

Even though Bob lost some good glasses, we found a great friend and everyone could see that.

Good music can also lift a laden heart as melodies flow and cares depart. Dad always enjoyed good harmony from his early days of singing with the Tiny Mike Trio in Reno to late night rendezvous with the voice of Perry Como in his living room chair. As the Hands of Time touched his brow, a tear was dried through song somehow. Now one tune that dad often sang to his own mama and papa was a moving melody that I call California Leavin'. For years, he encouraged Grandma Ann and Grandpa Earnie to move from the fertile yet seismically sown hills of California and join us in the dry bones desert of Nevada. In 1977, they waved a fond goodbye to Burbank and their pleasant cottage on East Orange Grove. I embraced dad's folks anew, who came to live with us for a season as we built them a nice home nearby.

Time continued to surge forward as George and I cruised on to see a new movie called Star Wars. In a galaxy far away, I became Obi-Don-Kenobi and a force to be reckoned with. If our starship ever broke down, Sam and I were already enrolled in auto shop and could probably fix it in a light year or less. Each new frame of bowling pins now became a challenging set of stormtroopers. I vigorously swept them away as a senior letterman with the high school bowling team. At seventeen, I gathered stars from beyond the sun and set them brightly in our universe of one. Old Blue Eyes was right, it was a very good year. The road to graduation was now complete and a time of new beginnings dawned before us. It was more than special to hear mother and dad cheer as I grasped a diploma trimmed in gold. Sam also received great applause as he stepped forward in the electric moment. Everyone then gave a resounding hurrah for the heroic parents who helped bring us there.

In 1979, the world became a better place as bouncing baby Sean slid across a hospital home base. Phyllis and George's first child made me an uncle as I bestowed chocolate treats upon everyone. Mother and dad were promoted to grandparents and delighted with their new roles of honor. Mother frequently stayed with Sean as he quickly grew and sang to him a happy song as only she could do. Little Seanie Boofer is My Sweetheart became a household favorite and topped the charts for many years to come.

Now time had turned Grandad E.L. Wilson's hair a soft silver and his heart to pure gold. A few months after Sean's birth, it also brought him home. Grandad stepped through a thin boundary of time on August 24, 1979. The rainbow of flowers that soon filled his and Mimi's home was just a small reflection of the dear man we had always known. It was graduation day for Grandad and he received a standing ovation above. In 1980, I began two years of volunteer service in Germany and met wonderful people at every hand. As I continued to learn the language, a nice lady asked me about Regan, which was the German word for rain. I observed blue skies above and couldn't find a cloud in sight. I then realized she was asking about President Reagan and not the kind for which you may need an umbrella. It was easy to love people from around the world and I missed them greatly upon returning home.

Phyllis and George welcomed two more little ones to join their merry crew. Brei and Noelle arrived as bright feathers from above on wings of peaceful doves. Now Grandpa Earnie sailed a strong and steady course from the very time his ship left port. Through tempest seas and tranquil nights, he bravely manned a valiant boat. Many a mate he lifted up with comforting hands of hope. His days now filled and work complete, a rainbow waved him home. Earnest Michael Brady reached a bay of perfect bliss on October 26, 1986. Each new generation seemed to quickly grow and thrive as thirsty red oaks in the rich ground of life. Mother and I brought nine year old Sean to some lake islands for a day of scientific discovery. He rambled along a rocky shore and found more forms of life than Jacques Cousteau. Even a camouflaged sunfish was briefly held for observation, then happily let go. Every odyssey of good experience brings fiber to a soul. It helps each life feel more complete, happy, rich and whole.

Grandma Ann saw many generations in her flowing fabric of time. She also received many awards and ribbons as a youthful Scottish Highland dancer growing up in Glasgow. Some of the kindest smiles she ever received were from wounded World War 1 soldiers as she lifted their spirits with a royal sword dance in hospitals of recovery. She volunteered countless times during a long life of service and still thought of others when almost 95. At a humble bedside, I briefly held her tired hand. Suddenly, she spoke with peaceful clarity.

Oh honey, there will be plenty of time to do all the things we want to do later on.

Ann Gilliland Scott Brady saw something beautiful on February 17, 1999.

She glanced once more and smiled goodbye, then danced across a golden sky.

When Angels Call

Go west, young man, go west. Dad felt inspired to move further west in the expanding Las Vegas Valley of 2003. Though his youthful hair and chiseled looks had gradually been transformed through time, his spirit was strong and yearned to climb. The home we built 30 years before was filled with a trainload of memories and moving on tugged at every heart in tow. Mother and I prepared the granddaddy of all garage sales to help make way for the great move. Their newer home in Sun City Summerlin was a snug yet cozy fit for a couple in the warm siesta of life.

In the autumn of 2005, I began to feel unusually tired as if having run a long race. My own Indy car seemed low on fuel yet trying to reach a distant finish line. Sometime in early December, I found myself in a transformative dream of the night. I walked from a building and stepped into the bright sunlight of day. Suddenly, I was above and slightly behind the scene and observed as my physical self moved forward. I noticed a few people in front of me and someone to my right. I saw myself wearing dark sunglasses and somehow knew that I was blind. There was no emotional upset, just an objective understanding that I was physically blind. Upon waking, I looked around my room for a few moments and curiously wondered about the detailed dream.

Christmas Eve was a cheerful time as I visited mother and dad at their warm place. We opened a few presents, laughed and enjoyed each other's company. Everyone was older now and we savored the small moments together. I returned home that night and sat in a small room of reflection. A peaceful calm touched me as if a dear friend were near. Quiet words of counsel then entered an open door of my mind.

You're about to face a real challenge in life.

It's not going to be easy.

No matter what happens, don't give up.

What's going to happen? I asked the unseen friend.

It's something you've never faced before and I'll be with you.

Remember to never give up.

I wondered for several moments about what was going to happen, then rested for the night. About five days later, I woke as usual and put on some glasses which had accompanied me since first grade. A brown smoggy spot appeared in the right lens. I removed my glasses to clean them, but the spot was still there. I brushed my right eye, yet the murky spot was everywhere. This was unusual but maybe it would clear up after a while. The next day revealed an even larger area of obscured vision. I began writing a few goals for the new year but had to close one eye just to focus. My first goal now was to see an eye doctor, but they were closed on New Year's Day. By the time I zeroed in on an ophthalmologist's wall chart early the next morning, that large letter E appeared as a grey bowl of mashed potatoes. The doctor looked into my eyes with a bright light and declared there was so much inflammation of the optic discs that I needed to see a better eye specialist right away. Within hours, an excellent ophthalmologist dilated and peered into my weary eyes. He gave a deep sigh and explained that I had extensive inflammatory damage to both optic nerves and would need immediate brain imaging and a CT scan of the orbits. He diagnosed me with acute optic neuritis and began a series of questions.

Did anyone in my family ever have multiple sclerosis?

How much eye pain did I feel?

Did my jaw hurt?

Any loss of appetite?

Actually, I'm pretty hungry right now.

Me too, the doctor smiled.

On the way home, I made a quiet and heartfelt request.

Please God, help me still be able to see and not loose all sight.

I visited my folks but didn't want to worry them and said I was having some difficulty seeing. Dad then searched for and found an eye patch in his drawer that I had worn at age five to help correct a weak eye muscle. He offered to cover my right eye to help it get better. I thanked him and explained this was a little different than weak eye muscles and involved the optic nerves. His kind concern however was some of the best medicine available. The CT scan revealed enlarged optic nerve sheaths surrounded by excessive cerebrospinal fluid. A quiet insight then came to mind. This process would affect the breathing. I took a deep breath which seemed normal.

That's about to change, came a soft whisper.

Two weeks later, I woke with shallow breathing and felt as if I had just climbed Mt. Everest. Both lower legs were weak and I was off-balance. My eyes were sensitive to light and both ears were ringing.

What was happening?

Each day seemed to bring a new symptom. I squinted at the incredible brightness of sunlight. Somehow the vision in my left eye was still fairly good. The ophthalmologist was surprised that I could still see through one eye as he again examined both optic nerves and described significant scarring. My left ear became so sensitive to sound that if someone's cell phone rang nearby, it sent shock waves through my body. Even the creak of a door provided more of a jolt than five cups of coffee ever could. Electric shock waves raced through my right arm and left leg in days that followed. A profound fatigue wrapped my entire body and just wouldn't leave. Any rest was welcome and brought some relief. As I drifted off, a dream began when a man stood at the foot of my bed.

You may lose the use of your legs, he said.

He then touched each lower leg as if to give them strength and help me endure. I soon awoke with a greater sense of well-being and increased energy.

I visited some new doctors in the weeks that followed with hopes their specialized experience could help determine what may have happened to my now unhappy body. Some good tests were done but most doctors were baffled. I asked about the possibility of multiple sclerosis or stroke and shared some perhaps helpful insights. It seemed that my unusual condition didn't wear a clear name tag and was becoming more of a mystery diagnosis.

Now dad always had a firm hand grip, but in the spring of 2006 that sure grasp began to fade. His resilient frame of determined strength now leaned with age as a weathered oak. A lifetime of prospecting his valley of chosen dreams, suddenly brought a sunset and full circle complete. Dad was hospitalized in July as the tide of his health ebbed further away. I sat by his bed and held that oft mighty man as a burst of effort then squeezed my sorrowful hand. He was still determined to make a brave and valiant stand.

Please God, help dad have great peace and special passage to a beautiful place.

The next day his hand lay still amid labored breathing. I quietly closed the hospital room door and gently held him near.

Dad, do you know how much you're loved?

Thank you for everything you did for me and all of us.

Do you realize how much you're loved?

A small puddle of tears formed beside him as my heart wept within.

We'll be together again soon where all cares are washed away.

You'll always be my friend, I whispered.

A quiet feeling came as I left the hospital that night.

Your father is going home now, but you'll see him again, I promise.

I visited mother and gave her a long hug.

I'm going to need your help, especially now she said.

We'll always be here for you mother.

I returned home and sat thinking about the past couple days when someone softly spoke.

Bye – bye.

I paused and realized it was dad.

A feeling then came that he had somehow heard every word expressed to him in the hospital room even though his physical body couldn't respond.

I rested about four hours until the phone rang. Dad passed that morning of July 12, 2006 as his earthly journey was complete.

Red, white and blue carnations adorned dad's ceremony, celebrating his patriotic service to Our Country and the love we felt for him. I sang a few hearty verses of Anchors Aweigh as dad's naval memories sailed majestically by. Phyllis, Linda and I each spoke and tried to touch upon his lifetime of adventure in just a few moments. An organist played one of dad's favorite melodies, that of Danny Boy. Scottish bagpipers then accompanied us to the Southern Nevada Veterans Memorial Cemetery in Boulder City. Our uniformed bagpipers marched forward with a resounding chorus of Amazing Grace that brought even cemetery residents to full attention. Mother was presented with a folded flag of honor as dad was laid to rest. But we hadn't heard the last from William J. Brady. You see, dad now had a new voice as another gallant leg of his eternal voyage began.

I visited mother more often following dad's passing and helped her with everyday things. She was always glad to see me as we encouraged each other. Then dad began to communicate even without a physical body or use of a cell phone. He first spoke in a dream.

They took me to a valley, he recounted with surprise.

Though I didn't initially see him, the voice was unmistakable as he described being met by those who guided him in the afterlife to a remarkable valley. Later, dad appeared in a supersensory dream wearing all white and surrounded by a degree of light. He looked the same as in life, only better. A full head of dark hair now accented his invigorated appearance. Dad described his process of passing to have been like a tornado, though I'm not exactly sure what that meant. Yet another time, mother sat on her sofa and suddenly described hearing dad.

Jay is talking to me. He's glad to be where he's at and doesn't want to come back!

Well, according to dad, I guess the grass really is greener on the other side.

Through a multitude of health challenges, I continued to see a few doctors with mixed results. If only they felt the same fire within that I did to find answers. Several nights I awoke with difficulty breathing, sometimes gasping for air. It felt like inflammation was ever present throughout my body. Mother and I still found occasion to laugh almost daily. Sometimes I challenged her in the grocery store parking lot to a footrace for the front door. She would give a few hops, then surrender in a cloud of giggles.

I just get too tickled, she laughed.

As I pushed a shopping cart through the aisles, my legs felt like having just run a double marathon.

You go ahead mother. I'll find a bench and sit for a while.

Fortunately, a See's Candy store was nearby and we found their chocolate treats to be a good remedy for many things.

Mother and I returned to Willow Beach where every wave seemed so familiar and warmed by yesterday's sun. Her lucky fishing hat bobbed gently as she surveyed a peaceful shoreline. I set mother's fishing chair among riverside rocks with a panoramic view of the pleasant hills nearby. A delicious morsel of rainbow Power Bait with glitter dangled from her eager line as she cast it beyond the quiet shore. Within moments, she felt a nibble and tug.

I think he's on, she excitedly said.

Keep reeling mother, keep reeling.

A shimmering rainbow trout jumped a half-circle around her feet as she lifted it ashore.

You did it mother, what a nice fish.

She looked at the colorful trout and into my still blue eyes with a smile that swept every worry aside. We brought seven trout home from the river that day, yet carried a lighter load along the way.

Now Wanda's mother Alma, or Mimi as we often called her, celebrated almost a century of life. She crossed the heart of Texas in rustic covered wagons, then saw a pair of Lamborghinis later cruise on by. She fixed the creaky windmill in July of '39 and watched a shuttle liftoff that roared through space and time. She fried those chicken gizzards with tender juicy care and cheered for every Cowboys game from a worn old rockin chair. Alma saw so many rainbows, each dipped in heaven's gold, then sat upon the brightest one as angels called her home.

Alma Lorene Johnson Wilson lifted off for the ride of her life on February 17, 2007 for that joyous journey from here to heaven.

In 2008, mother encouraged me to come live at her place.

I'm glad when you're here, why don't you stay, she insisted.

I accepted her invitation and found welcome rest in the extra room. It was good to be with mother as we walked through fields of memory still bright with the sunflowers of June.

Remember how you washed my hair in the small kitchen sink at Indian Springs?

You were my little boy, she smiled.

We can't forget when I drew on the face of Linda's Howdy Doody doll with all those colored markers. I thought it was great fun until trying to wash off what turned out to be permanent marker.

Mother, I have a confession to make.

Go ahead, she grinned.

One time I found a box of mixed Halloween candy hidden under your bed. Each day I secretly returned and liberated a few more treats until only some Tootsie Rolls remained, then I ate them too. I want to repent now.

She chuckled and waved with a twinkle that set my spirit free.

I enjoyed helping mother with a variety of errands and continued to drive though only able to see well through one eye. Some things appeared to be off-center when actually straight and depth perception could also be a challenge. I guess the local baseball team wouldn't have considered me a top pick for most positions.

A strange phenomenon then began to occur as I lay my head on a pillow each night. A brief jolt surged through my head as scattered flashes of blue light appeared. It was rather startling at first, but I soon prepared myself for the unexplained evening event. I described the new symptoms to some doctors who were still perplexed. A bright rash enveloped two fingers of my left hand and both feet were constantly cold. Some clear impressions came but finding full answers was like searching for gold.

A familiar voice spoke in June of 2010 and said another challenge was about to begin.

What could it be? I wondered.

Pray that angels will be with you, especially now, the whisper continued.

I secretly bowed my head and did as the prompting said.

Further insight quickly came.

You'll need to go to a hospital soon.

I considered a possible reason but didn't understand why.

Two days later, I awoke with a humming sound in my head. As I opened my good left eye, a solid rectangle of blackness appeared. Moments of great concern swept my mind as the possibility of further optic neuritis flashed anew. I carefully made way for a door and watched as the black box in my vision gradually turned pink and somewhat normal. I called the kind ophthalmologist whose staff instructed me to come in right away. With a worried look, he carefully examined each eye and optic nerve.

I don't see any new inflammation, he said with relief, but call my emergency number if there are any more changes.

A welcome feeling set in as I still wondered about the dramatic developments from just a few hours earlier.

Mother and I sat at home as I assured her things would be alright.

I'm worried about you Donnie and know that you're not well.

Thank you, mother. It's ok, I'll be fine.

Within hours, the once clear images of my good left eye began to flicker like a stuttering movie projector. I picked up a large book and turned the first page. Several lines of print simply vanished from view. I slowly moved a hand in front of my face but could only see three fingers. Where were the other two?

I called the eye doctor and described what was happening.

Get to a hospital right away, he instructed.

You've got optic neuritis again and must try to save what vision remains.

Mother, I'm going to a hospital and may be gone for a while.

I'll be alright and will call you tonight.

Maybe I'll meet a cute nurse there who checks my blood pressure.

Gosh, I'm excited already.

Here, give me a hug before I go.

Please be careful, you're still my little boy.

A pleasant nurse greeted me at the emergency room.

What can we do for you today?

I'm having some difficulty seeing things, I explained.

Let me ask you a few questions, she continued.

When did you first notice a problem with your eyes?

About 4 ½ years ago, I replied.

How do your legs feel?

They've been weak for about 4 ½ years.

What about your breathing?

Haven't been able to get a full breath of air for some time.

How long have you been experiencing this?

About 4 ½ years, I winked.

What about your ears and hearing?

They're both ringing.

When did that start? she grinned.

About 4 ½ years ago.

Well, you're just a train wreck, she proclaimed with an incurable smile.

Yes, but maybe a fixable one, I laughed.

Ok, follow me, she said.

I gladly lay on a hospital bed for a few moments of rest as other nurses and lab techs circled nearby. The ceiling lights seemed brighter than a supernova as everything else grew dim. A doctor appeared and began asking more questions.

When did this all begin?

About 4 ½ years ago, but a day or so with the good left eye.

He noticed the fire engine red rash on my left hand and offered to treat that also. A couple calls were made and on we rolled for treatment to try and save some vision. Strong intravenous steroids began coursing through my system to perhaps slow the powerful inflammatory process that now gripped my body. Each hour my vision grew dimmer and both upper legs felt weak. A neurologist came by that night and confirmed a diagnosis of acute optic neuritis. My remaining sight was being swept away in a hurricane of inflammation. In a dim and silent hospital room, I quietly sought help from the friend who always seemed to be there.

Please God, keep giving me strength to go forward and make the best of whatever may come.

The next day a doctor returned and extended a compassionate hand towards mine.

I'm sorry, but you'll need immune suppressing drugs for the rest of your life.

Thank you doctor, whatever happens I'll be alright.

Following three days of high dose steroid treatment, I returned home and was glad to visit with mother.

The ophthalmologist examined both eyes again and gave somber news. The inflammation had subsided but left severe damage and further vision loss in its wake. Thankfully, just enough partial and washed out vision remained to prevent complete blindness. Bumping into door frames now became common and guessing the numbers on a phone was difficult. Deciphering letters on a computer keyboard seemed impossible. Yet, it's not what happens to us in life, but what we make of it that matters. Mother had a glossy red four wheeled walker that we called Ruby. I could still tell it was red though not clearly. The identity of several colors became somewhat of a guess and others more of a mystery. Everything I could partially see became more beautiful.

I yearned for the ability to drive again and tried to walk more often as hurried cars sped by. Everywhere I went now required caution as I listened for approaching vehicles but couldn't always see them coming. Mother encouraged me to get a blind cane which I hesitated to do.

People don't realize you can't see but many would if you had a white cane, she explained. Mother was right, so I got a small white cane with a red stripe and named him Baxter. He was better than a dog and went with me to the store and for everyday walks. His elastic wristband was like a happy tail that always wagged as we went somewhere together. Baxter liked to make friends and people often held a door open for us as we visited new places. I still enjoyed walking in the neighborhood even though my legs always felt tired.

Remember to take Bax with you and be careful, mother reminded me.

I love you mother and will come back soon.

I love you Donnie.

Her face looked like an angel in the soft warm light.

I guess mothers often appear that way in this journey we call life.

A Bouquet Of Memories

Mother often walked with Ruby to a favorite indoor oasis. The pastel living room sofa offered a comfortable place to rest and caress the velvet pages of life. Her mind danced through meadows of memory as she embraced earlier years and special friendships. I savored the moments as Wanda led me along precious pathways of time.

Alma and E.L. Wilson raised three lovely girls on a small rural farm near Wellington, Texas. Margie Louise was their first, arriving on December 2, 1927. Wanda Nell joined them on November 11, 1931 and Wilma Janell completed their crown on May 12, 1934. Wanda cheerfully recalled her third birthday with bright clarity. She stood atop a large clothing trunk and happily announced – Today I am Three! The first day of school, little Wanda Nell wondered what her new adventure might bring. She walked the old school road swinging her lunch pail round and round. Later, she opened the lunch her mother had carefully made to find cottage cheese somehow covered everything.

Now Wilma, her younger sister, was born with a smile. Together they played house as Mr. and Mrs. Brown. Most of the time, Wanda talked Wilma into playing the part of Mr. Brown. The fresh mud pies they made always baked well under a Texas Panhandle sun. They climbed in wooden barrels and rolled down hills of fun, rode spirited stick ponies as far as they could run. They watched a windmill turn in time and heard its sacred song as cheerful birds rose above a rainbow just beyond. Many of the clothes they wore were handmade by Alma. Such was the beautiful white satin dress and sky blue sash that Wanda wore as Victory Queen of her school class in 1942. Her grandmother Bertha once wrote on a picture postcard, "this is Wanda Nell, isn't she lovely" and truly she was. Wonderful times were also shared with Wanda's cousin Wilsie. They ran across sunflower fields covered by blue skies that swept on forever. Every sunset seemed like God's own signature of approval. Even the night sky was illuminated with imagination. Wanda and Wilsie watched as fireflies glowed amidst them and the stars. They caught several in Miracle Whip jars, then released them back into the rich tapestry of night.

Wanda's folks planted several crops on their country farm. Each growing season and time of year brought new harvest. Her daddy would load the wagon with watermelon and grapes they had grown. Some horses pulled them into town where people eagerly approached the bountiful offering. Ripe red watermelon or a bucket of grapes for ten cents, everyone was glad. Wanda's Grandaddy Elbert often came by the farm for a visit. With pep in his voice he resolutely said, "Gal, if I'd a seen you in town, I'd have got you an ice cream."

Well, he actually saw me several times in town that day, Wanda recalled.

Mother, let me get you that bowl of ice cream now. You've been waiting long enough.

Chocolate or strawberry?

Maybe a little of both.

Almost 70 years and miles of memory later, she found it just as sweet.

Time to wake up mother, this is your hair day.

Go away and let me sleep.

We already have an appointment for you to see the hair lady.

Change it, I want to sleep.

Mother, a driver is already coming to pick you up. I can help you get ready.

You're the meanest man in the whole world, she declared.

Mother began to say some funny things, but I smiled just the same.

There's some breakfast ready for you in the kitchen, then you can brush your teeth.

That's what's wrong with you, you're always wanting me to brush my teeth, she fussed.

People need to brush their teeth, mother.

No they don't, she insisted.

Reminding mother to do things had recently become somewhat of a fun wrestling match.

Now that you're ready, let's wait a while in the living room.

Mother and I often enjoyed sitting and looking through a sliding glass door onto the patio. Where we lived in Sun City, colorful quail and cute cottontail rabbits were plentiful.

Let's sit and watch the little creatures, mother whispered.

Excited quail quickly emerged from the brush and scurried towards the glass door as if someone had just rung a lunch bell. Maybe it was the tasty sunflower seeds we cast their way.

Here mother, cup your hands together as I pour in some kernels for the quail.

Now give them a good toss across the patio.

Our hearty band of quail echoed their unanimous approval.

Mother, can you see any rabbits?

Yes, let's give them some food, they're hungry too, she said.

Ok, pitch some of these baby carrots out there.

Here come the Sun City Rabbits!

On first base was Ears, an older rabbit that mother had named. A young family of cottontails was near second base with Eddie Rabbitt in centerfield. Another pair stayed around third base where they were … well, making more rabbits. I guess our fluffy friends enjoyed their bright orange treats as much as we did watching them.

Mother's driver soon arrived and I helped her settle in for a comfortable ride.

We'll see you ladies in a while, after you're all beautified.

Upon returning indoors, I noticed the patio slider had been left open just a bit. One of the Gambel's quail had also seen this and decided to further introduce himself.

You'll enjoy things much more outside, I told the curious bird.

A gentle approach was made to fully open the sliding door and make way for his flight to freedom. Our new guest took flight towards the kitchen instead. There he made a presidential landing atop a runway of cabinets.

Wouldn't you like to go outside? I asked the dignified guest.

He stood there sincerely considering my request.

I explained to him the many benefits of outdoor living, the almost unlimited flight miles he could accrue and a variety of outdoor events to simply enjoy. He walked back and forth along the upper cabinets–considering, reconsidering and waffling like a seasoned politician. Suddenly, he took flight to a yet greater vantage point, enthroning himself upon the pinnacle of our china cabinet. This bird had an IQ of 214! I reasoned with him, pointing towards an open door and freedom, even offering a full pardon. We sat and negotiated for several minutes, each thinking the other unreasonable. Finally, mother and her driver returned – advantage humans.

We have a new guest, I informed them.

What shall we call our regal friend?

Let's name him Dan, I suggested. Dan Quail.

Everyone agreed and confirmed it so.

Now, how could we help Dan?

I thought of my long-handled fishing net which successfully landed so many striped bass.

Could you gals guide me as I lift the net up towards Dan?

You're almost there, keep going, he's in the net! they hollered.

Well, lucky Dan got first class service to the great outdoors and a blue sky destination of his choice. I couldn't see where Dan flew but somehow knew he would come back soon … for more of those nutrient rich sunflower seeds that made him so smart.

An unexpected telegram arrived one morning in the form of a high definition dream. Mother's face suddenly appeared and drew ever near. I felt the word Alzheimer's and quietly awoke. A sense of what perhaps lay ahead entered my mind. Would mother develop Alzheimer's? Hopefully not, but something seemed to indicate the possibility. A routine doctor appointment for mother had already been scheduled and would perhaps be a good time for an all-around evaluation. Now I had recently gone to the kitchen and couldn't remember why I was there. Maybe I could use some kind of evaluation. Eventually, I gently asked mother how she felt about her memory.

Pretty good, she thought.

Can you ask your doctor during the next visit to look into your beautiful memory?

Ok, she smiled.

The physician visit and results were fine, but subtle things began to occur as the months went by. Sometimes mother would ask the same question during a brief conversation or seem to forget something previously mentioned. I helped more with everyday things as heartfelt concerns continued. A further physician follow-up indicated no serious memory problem but to return regularly as we did.

Mother and I often walked together in the twilight of summer days and guessed how many rabbits we might see along the way. Her keen eyes became expert at spotting quiet cottontails along the brush lined greenbelt. Yet as summer ebbed, so did the strength of my body. Radiant starburst sensations rippled through both legs like a choreographed fireworks display. Holding a small cup caused each arm to feel weary. The effort to breathe felt like rowing a boat as sinuses filled with much of Lake Mead. Kleenex quickly became my new best friend. Whatever was pulling my health out to sea, perhaps my body could somehow mend.

Let's wash your hair, mother.

Here's a pitcher of warm water, some shampoo and a nice towel.

Everything's ready for you in the kitchen.

There's also some red velvet cake for you in the fridge after we're done.

Are you really going to give me some cake or just saying that?

Yes mother, I'll bring it to you on Ruby.

Soapy, soapy, she said, as we washed and rinsed again.

Keep your eyes closed just a little longer.

There, now dry your hair while I get Ruby.

Donnie, could you clean my glasses?

Sure mother, can you see better now?

Oh yes, you did a good job.

Well, I believe there were enough fingerprints on those glasses to prove they were yours.

Mother laughed as I rolled Ruby up to her sofa. Now Ruby was more than just a trusted walker, she served as a great tv tray on wheels. Mother looked on eagerly as a perfect square of red velvet cake was set before her. In that moment, I remembered how a young mother had washed the hair of a small boy at the kitchen sink and given him a special treat. Just then, mother looked up with a kind smile and said, "You're my little boy."

An autumn breeze swirled among rose colored leaves as mother reached to remember simpler things. Her gaze became distant when time drifted by, as if watching a kite as it floated in flight.

Donnie, can you fix my tv?

I'll sure try, mother.

She then handed me a remote with more functions than an airplane cockpit. There were green buttons, red ones, blue and white squares, arrows pointing in every direction. You almost needed a master's degree to figure how things worked. There was even a remote for the remote control. Greatly diminished vision brought further challenge.

Let's see mother, where's the power button? That works.

It's asking what language you want to speak.

Would you like to learn Espanol?

I always wanted to speak French.

Eventually, we made it to a tv channel menu and an incredible number of viewing options. You could watch and learn how to plant a garden, one of my favorites. You could travel to far away places like Juneau, Alaska or Barstow, California. If you were really hungry and didn't have much food in the house, there was a channel about barbequing every kind of delicious food you could desire. People would even taste it for you and describe how good it was. As I sat on the couch nibbling some potato chips, another channel featured an athletic person surrounded by several admirers.

Do you want to look like this? a voice asked.

Yes, I replied.

Well, you can!

For just 3 easy payments of $49 we'll send you more photos of people like this and your own personal jump rope. But that's not all – act now and we'll also send you a free bonus video about how to do sit ups. Now if you ever experience insomnia, there's a governmental proceedings channel that can cure it faster than any known medication.

There were so many tv channels, but mother just wanted to watch Little House on the Prairie, which was probably the best choice.

Ok mother, I think everything works now.

Oh, thank you Donnie, you're my good boy.

Some people just have a natural ability to cook and prepare good food. I seem to lack this talent and always kept a couple fire extinguishers near the kitchen. Mother and I enjoyed easy to make cuisine and a variety of deli sandwiches topped our tasty menu.

Mother, would you like some BLT, chicken salad and tuna sandwiches for dinner?

Yes I would, she quickly replied.

I'll call a driver and go pick some up from our favorite place.

I'll only be gone a little while. Will you be alright till I get back?

Yes Donnie, I'll be just fine.

Ok, give me a hug. Stay here and don't go outside with Ruby.

Mother gave an assuring smile as the driver came by.

We arrived at the sandwich shop where I placed and received our order. Right then, an urgent feeling came over me and I turned to the driver.

I need to get home right away.

I don't know why but something has happened.

Get there safely but please hurry.

The driver was rather surprised and we sped back home.

As we arrived and pulled up front, the driver made a startling discovery.

There's someone laying in the yard, he declared.

It's your mother!

Near the sidewalk and among some rugged rocks was the silhouette of a body.

I jumped from the vehicle and shouted within – Please God, don't let mother be dead!

Mother are you ok?

I called again while rushing towards a figure that lay face down and motionless.

Then a muffled but familiar voice spoke.

I've fallen and can't get up you idiot.

What relief to hear those words and hold those beautiful hands again.

I'm going to call for help, just lay still mother.

As rescue was on the way, I gently asked why she left the indoor safety of home.

I just wanted to see where you were, she said.

The medics and I carefully stabilized and turned mother right side up.

Someone found Ruby in the distance after she almost rolled away.

Mother, I'm so glad you're alright. Let's go to a hospital where they can make sure you're ok.

The paramedics raised mother into the back of an ambulance as I sat up front.

That's my son – he's blind, she told them.

One of the medics then noticed my white cane Baxter beside me.

Mother, the medics need to put an IV in your arm, but they'll be gentle.

Just then she howled.

Take that thing out you idiot!

Mother has a memory condition, I whispered to one of them.

Don't feel bad, she called me an idiot too. It's just the Alzheimer's talkin.

Our journey brought us to a hospital where I requested comprehensive scans and testing for any possible injury. Thankfully, all test results came back normal. The doctors and I both suggested a further night of observation would be good.

The taxi ride home seemed to travel through time. The events from hours earlier felt as if they occurred long ago. I walked with Baxter towards a blurry yet welcome porch light. There at the front door I found Ruby, as if waiting for a best friend. She already missed mother and so did I.

It was a bright morning when mother came home and my heart was fully glad. There would be further visits to a hospital, or as Grandpa Earnie called it, a day at the Country Club. Every plateau on our journey brought new horizons of understanding and compassion. Mother now lay quietly on her sofa, warmly wrapped in a plush comforter. She curiously gazed across the room at a colorful box and decorative bow.

What's that? she suddenly asked.

A box of Rocky Mountain Chocolates that Phyllis sent for Christmas.

Her eyes began to twinkle as if a marvelous event was about to unfold.

Let's eat them, she whispered.

That's a good idea, I softly said.

Can you guess what flavor each one is?

Chocolate always seemed to be her favorite answer.

Mother then looked towards something new in the living room.

What's that? she secretly asked.

A Christmas teddy bear just brought home, I smiled.

Can we play with it? she tenderly asked.

Yes, mother.

When I was five, mother gave me a soft aqua blue dolphin called Flipper for Christmas. He could make special sounds and cheerful calls whenever I asked him. Sometimes I would fall asleep holding Flipper close to me.

I gently placed the smiling bear in mother's wrinkled hands.

What would you like to name her?

She carefully looked at her new friend, then quietly caressed the soft face and blue velvet dress.

Dolly, she glowingly said.

That's a good name, mother.

Hold Dolly and keep her safe.

She lay her head on a pillow and held Dolly nigh.

Mother's eyes began to close as soft light glowed nearby.

A bright bouquet of memories graced the gentle night

As harps of home played a tune that touched her heart and mine.

Where Rainbows Begin

January first was always a day of new beginnings. On this new day of 2013, I lay down and closed my eyes for a brief rest. A deep sleep then touched my hand as a scene unfurled and dream began. Mother appeared wearing a beautiful white dress and purple sash around the waist, which streamed along her side. The sash signified that mother was a precious member of heaven's royal family. She lovingly looked at me and said, "I need to go now." Then another lady wearing a similar white dress, who seemed to be a special guide, came and stood by mother's side. Gradually, they turned and went somewhere together. I awoke thinking of mother and wondering where I was. Upon remembering it was the first day and beginning of a new year, a quiet feeling whispered in my heart that mother would be going home soon.

Mother, how was your lunch?

The roast beef was good and the frosted carrot cake even better, she grinned.

I rolled Ruby aside as mother relaxed on the sofa again.

She then reached for my hand and held it as only a mother could.

Will you take care of me? she quietly asked.

Yes mother, the best I can.

A wide smile then brushed her face as sunlight touched her resting place.

The time may come that you'll need round the clock care.

If so, I'll search for a nice place that specializes in giving full-time care.

I want to stay with you, she softly said.

I want to be with you too, mother.

Maybe that time won't come, but if it does, heaven will let both of us know and I'll come see you every day.

I know you're not well, Donnie.

It's ok mother, the doctors I've seen just aren't sure what to do.

I have an appointment to see another doctor on Friday and maybe should ask him to just put me down, I reasoned aloud.

Oh don't say that, she exclaimed with a worried look.

Well, even a family pet that you love may have been unwell for quite some time and it's best to have the ailing dog put down, I continued.

Maybe I'll just ask the doctor to put me down.

No, don't say that! Listen, you're the best dog I ever had, she declared.

Ok mother, I won't do it.

I gently held her hand and explained it was all fun as a welcome smile of relief beamed from her face once more.

Early blossoms of February appeared along our walkway as a first breath of spring drew near. Some zesty songbirds celebrated the promise of each new day with their fanciful versions of reveille. Warm days were always welcome but something had changed. My body now became weak from sunlight itself. The very rays of life had become like kryptonite. Once strong muscles grew weaker by the moment as solar rashes appeared. Even the tops of my ears turned red like ripe chili peppers in a southwestern sun. Just putting on tennis shoes and tying them took great effort. It was then that I went for a walk across what soon became my Sahara Desert. The first few minutes were tolerable, but the accumulated sands of the past seven years' condition suddenly weighed upon my whole body with each exhausting step. My tired lungs wrestled with every breath as both legs felt like giant Sequoia trees lumbering forward. Something fluttered in my chest as every ounce of effort was summoned to carry on.

Please God, give me strength to make it home.

It's affecting your heart now, a quiet voice whispered.

One more step, now another, keep going. Just focus on each step.

Somehow, I made it and reached the cool oasis of a bed at home. When I awoke, several hours had passed but something felt different. I struggled to open my eyes as profound exhaustion lingered. Again, I drifted away, this time until the next day and a place of partial recovery.

I had wondered for some time if my ongoing health challenges were the result of an autoimmune process in the body. Could a powerful autoimmune train have somehow left an inner station and was still hurtling along a wrong way track? Something was wreaking havoc in my body as I tried to hold it back. Perhaps my own immune system that once protected me had become a determined storm of friendly fire.

Fortunately, I found a supportive doctor who was glad to join a positive quest for diagnosis and understanding. Further specialized tests were done, some of which I requested myself. The antinuclear antibody or ANA lab test can be helpful in recognizing possible autoimmune conditions. Though not conclusive, it offers a good window for viewing autoimmune indicators. A few days before the test results and follow-up visit, some new insight arrived. A doctor spoke in a vivid dream and explained that I had lupus. The phrase "types of lupus" was then emphasized. The doctor was surrounded by medical charts and results that seemed to confirm the diagnosis. Upon waking, I wondered what lupus really was. I'd heard of the condition but knew nothing about it. A few days later, I sat in an exam room waiting for the physician to enter. A door quietly opened as the doctor came in.

Here's the deal … you've got lupus, he said.

The ANA test was positive as were several other criteria.

Well, at least we know what it is, I nodded.

Yet, this was not a standard case of lupus, if ever there were such a thing. Somehow, I knew in my heart that this was lupus with a twist, an unusual lemon twist. The central nervous, vascular, muscular, endocrine, skeletal, cardiovascular and respiratory systems were all affected. Only my taste buds seemed to answer a wellness roll call. It's often good to work with your strengths, so I counseled with my physician about beginning an intensive course of Ben and Jerry's ice cream therapy.

You know, hope is a lovely gateway that can always frame tomorrow. Perhaps the answer isn't always in the answer, but in a journey to it.

April soon arrived with a gift basket of blossoms that caused every heart to sing. Orange, lavender, pink, red and yellow were sprinkled around almost everything. A pastel pink crepe myrtle tree stood especially bright in the sunny front yard. It had weathered many storms and become a favorite home for hummingbirds. Mother loved hummingbirds and each year we noticed a new or refurbished nest in the tree. Great activity and dazzling flights would often surround the crepe myrtle in spring. I'm not really sure what kind of sound hummingbirds make. I didn't hear them chirp and don't believe they quack, but you can sometimes hear their wings when hovering above your back. I guess they're kind of like angels.

Mother grew some orange and violet lantanas which seemed to flourish almost year round. Even after a frigid winter, they would come back with gorgeous new life. Our hummingbirds were especially drawn to the lush lantanas. Maybe they were attracted to vibrant colors or the unique auras that emanate from all living things. One of those beautiful creatures hovered near my face as I stood by the tree one day. Though unable to see the little bird, it was wonderful to hear and feel its presence.

Mother rested more as the days grew longer. I often walked with her from the sofa toward an ever glowing lamp in her room.

Keep going mother, you're almost there.

She smiled as I encouraged her forward.

Go to the light mother, go to the light.

Mother's condition continued to change as fewer current memories remained. One day, I heard the front door open and found her standing with Ruby as she gazed toward a far away place.

Are you looking for something, mother?

I'm going to get my little boy, she said.

It's alright mother, I'm here.

Let's go to your room where you can rest for a while.

A day or so later, a quiet message touched my ear.

It's time, a gentle voice said, the time is here.

Mother then emerged from her room. Someone was also talking to her.

What were they saying?

It's time, she echoed.

Someone was letting both of us know it was now time.

My heart was sad as I met with a doctor to discuss mother's future care. Yet somehow, we knew what was best for the friend we loved so dear. I accompanied mother to a nearby skilled nursing facility and visited her each day. The nurses waved as Baxter and I frequently patrolled the hallways leading toward her room. Seeing mother and hearing her voice was the best part of every day. One afternoon, mother sat in a wheelchair quietly waiting in the hall. As I approached from the distance, a familiar voice called out to me.

Keep going Donnie, keep going, she urged.

I followed the voice to find mother and hugged her for what seemed like forever. I helped feed her at lunch and sometimes brought special treats for dinner. Eventually, we prepared mother for transition to a full-time memory care center.

I looked toward mother's favorite sofa one night and around the quiet living room at home. Tears then came like a long summer rain and didn't clear for some time. Mother still seemed near as a swelling river of memories rushed by. The mother who always loved and cheered me on would someday soon be gone.

Please God, keep helping mother, she needs you so much now.

And when You're done, please help me too.

Mother entered memory care and received compassionate care for a challenging condition. The kind people who work and serve others in such facilities are special angels indeed. Mother and I sometimes sang together as summer days gathered in. Her simple rendition of Twinkle, Twinkle, Little Star seemed to illuminate each approaching night with perfect light. We sang Somewhere Over the Rainbow as whisperings of early autumn drew near.

What should we sing now, mother?

Birds fly over the rainbow, she chimed once more.

Mother, maybe I'll go with you over the rainbow this time.

Suddenly, a resolute tone filled her voice as she firmly held my hand.

You can't come yet, she kindly replied.

It almost seemed like someone was with us as we sang before waving goodbye.

A distant rain must have swept the sky as I returned home that day. I walked by the crepe myrtle tree and noticed something in a faint horizon. I was drawn to a towering arch and with great intent followed it across what seemed to be an open blue sky. It appeared to begin at the memory care center I had just left.

Don, look at that giant rainbow! a neighbor exclaimed.

Though I couldn't see the colors, it was just as beautiful to me.

That night, an emerald green hummingbird hovered before me as I slept. I didn't want the glistening bird to leave but it rose upward and was lifted away as I awoke. A call then came from the memory care center. Could I come quickly and see the doctor and nurses who were already there. Something had changed and mother was now passing away.

I stayed with mother for 2 ½ days as an unseen veil became thin. I ran out of kleenex and held her hand as kind attendants came in.

She's somehow holding on, a nurse explained.

It's ok to go mother.

Mimi and Grandad are waiting for you.

Everyone will be so glad to see you.

Some special visitors may come tonight and it's alright to go with them.

I love you so much and will see you again soon.

I cradled mother's head, kissed her cheek and said goodbye.

Even Boulder Dam couldn't hold back the tears as I left that night.

The phone rang just after midnight and I knew what the message was before answering. Mother had just gone home on a golden eye angel flight. More tears streamed from a dry river flow.

Well mother, did you go to the light? I softly asked.

Instantly, a spring of vibrant words entered my mournful heart.

Yes – did I ever!

A communication so natural and real continued as mother described having already met with God and of receiving a special promise. Suddenly, I could see mother with her own mother Mimi and knew they were together. A quickened sense of how rapidly things take place in heaven touched my mind. Then some clear and gentle words were softly heard.

You made my life worth living, someone whispered.

I wept again and it seemed like mother was really there as she hugged my aching heart.

Now a wonderful insight had unexpectedly come prior to mother's passing. As we leave the physical body, our spirit self seems to receive a heavenly transformation as we soon look and feel much younger. Mother appeared to be in her twenties and full of life. Maybe we can all look and feel that well up ahead.

It was a full day visiting the funeral home and preparing for the service to be held in Amarillo. Mother had asked me to bring her back to Texas where she could rest by Mimi and Grandad. By day's end, I was ready to lay my head on a deep pillow and quickly close my eyes. But someone had a special message to deliver that I was about to receive. Just as I closed my eyes to sleep, a spiritual voice began to speak. As if someone were calling through a giant megaphone, the intensity of each word grew with rolling crescendos.

Where do I sign up to say I love Donnie!

I was so startled by the resounding words that I almost jumped from bed.

In a moment or two, I realized who it was and answered the call.

Mother, I love you too.

I closed my eyes again and found a peaceful place. Somehow, I slept for a long time, perhaps a very long time.

Everyone embraced mother's memory at a beautiful service in Amarillo. My niece Brei and I sang Somewhere Over the Rainbow as fluttering leaves turned golden yellow. Our cousins Gail, Jan, Cindy and Alan kept us wrapped with Texas love that warmed each passing day.

The little girl who once ran through fields of summer flowers, now rests in the morning mist of quiet autumn showers. We didn't see any rainbows that clear October day. Perhaps mother had already made them all along the way.

Wanda Nell Wilson Brady touched the top of a brilliant rainbow October 11, 2013.

If you ask, I'm really not sure where every rainbow ends,
but maybe I can tell you where some of them begin.

Made in the USA
Columbia, SC
14 September 2020